Flowers, for Hitler

The Extraordinary Life
of Ilse Dorsch

◊ ◊ ◊

Flowers for Hitler

a true story

by
mike whicker

a Walküre imprint

ISBN: 978-0-9844160-7-3

printed in the United States of America

Reviews

As a lifelong student of history, and particularly military history, I believe this biography is a valuable addition to the rare, first-person accounts of German civilians who lived through the rise and fall of the Third Reich. Mike Whicker is to be commended for his persistence in pursuing and preserving this remarkable piece of eye-witness history. There are many lessons to be gleaned from the journey of Ilse Dorsch's life and transformation from a strident Hitler Youth member to contented American of deep spiritual faith.

— David Jones, Esq.

Flowers for Hitler is the personal account of a young German girl who came of age during Adolf Hitler's Third Reich. She became a loyal member of the Hitler Youth early in life and was indoctrinated into the Nazi culture, as were so many others at that time. This engrossing biography gives us a strong indication of what life was like for a female member of the Hitler Youth, as well as the "average" German, during the Hitler years. It is brilliantly written and is a must read for any student of history.

— Darrell Davis, historian

This is the powerful story of Ilse Dorsch, a girl growing up in a world dominated by a false prophet and his delusionary dreams. Through her young and impressionable eyes we see how an entire country can be led astray and subjugated by a powerful but evil elite through propaganda, misguided social engineering, and the threat of violence. We can also see the suffering that can be brought upon an entire country by an unwavering allegiance to a man consumed in a nationalistic ideal of his own imagination. Presented to us in this biography is the disillusionment the 'average' citizen of Germany experienced when finally the real truth was known. It is also a captivated story of personal redemption and rebirth in a new country. Most importantly, *Flowers for Hitler* is a first-hand account of a very important part of a larger history lesson that the world must never forget.

— David Gray, Esq.

Frequent readers of Mike Whicker's novels will see some much loved similarities in this true story, first-hand biography.

Whicker takes you "right there" from page one to the credit of the biography's subject, Ilse Dorsch. This is done through great attention to even the tiniest details.

Flowers for Hitler includes some enlightening information on some very high profile and well known people of the Third Reich—today we would call them "celebrities." And it is amazing that someone who rubbed shoulders with Hitler himself ended up in the small town of Mount Vernon, Indiana.

As an ex-German, (born and raised in Southern Germany – not far from Ilse's home) and now an American by choice, I can testify that the description of the time and situation is accurate and matches with what I have learned from my grandparents, including the public knowledge of the persecution of the Jews.

What we have here is an accurate record of history as it happened from the perspective of a person who lived through it. The twists and turns of Ilse's fate will not fail to astonish the reader. If you desire to get a better insight into the 'nuts and bolts' of the Third Reich, this is a must read.

— Detlef Alle

Most who have the tiniest interest in the past have read some histories of Hitler's Third Reich and the Nazi Party.

Flowers for Hitler: the Extraordinary Life of Ilse Dorsch is the true story of a little German girl who was filled with pride when she was chosen to present a bouquet to Adolf Hitler. By her own admission, Ilse grew up a loyal Nazi. She was programmed to believe that her country's Führer was the savior of her world. Yet her life would became so much more than being just a good little German Fräulein.

Whicker wrote *Flowers for Hitler* in first person from Ilse's point of view and it is a fascinating read. This book can easily be read in two sittings (if you can force yourself to put it down). Anyone with the slightest interest in WWII history will love this book.

— Kathy Pfettscher, Howard County (Indiana) Historical Society

For:
My three children
Roger, Connie and Maryhelen,
my eight grandchildren and thirteen great-grandchildren,
and also in memory of my husband Gene
and our son Danny.
— Ilse Horacek née Dorsch

Forward

I met Ilse Horacek née Dorsch in 2009 when she appeared at a book signing of my novel *Blood of the Reich* held at a German club in Evansville, Indiana. As I signed her book, she mentioned in passing that she grew up in the Third Reich, and that her father knew a man by the name of Karl Lehmann. This immediately got my full attention for two reasons. WWII historians worth their salt will jump at any chance to learn more about "average" Germans who lived during those years. And the fact her father knew the father of an infamous Nazi spy I've spent over twenty years of my life researching and writing about was something more I had to find out about. I asked Ilse for her phone number and called her a few days later.

Ilse was gracious enough to invite me to her home and it was there that I started learning a few bits and pieces of the incredible story that is Ilse's life. I knew right away that her story needed to be told— fascinating history like Ilse's should be preserved. I asked her to let me write her story but initially she refused. Eventually she relented to my never-ending onslaught, and because of that we have this book.

What follows is the personal account of a woman who has lived through the most mind-boggling era in modern times, and indeed perhaps of all time, the rise of Adolf Hitler's Third Reich.

The book is written in the first person from Ilse's point of view because it is her story in her words garnered from hours of taped interviews I conducted in her home, and from countless emails and telephone calls. Ilse saved many of her letters from those years and the letters included in the book are copied word for word.

What makes this biography unique is it covers the life and times of a *female* member of the Hitler Youth. A young girl who grew up in the culture of Nazi Germany, a culture that Ilse, along with so many others, believed in and supported during those times. But more importantly it is a biography of a young girl who had the inner strength to survive those times and hypnotic beliefs to become the adult you will meet in this book.

— Mike Whicker

Part 1

"He alone, who owns the youth, gains the future."

— Adolf Hitler

Chapter 1

The Bluest of Eyes

One of my earliest memories is from the summer of 1934. Indeed, it is a memory I think would be difficult for anyone to forget, even at the tender age of four.

It was a warm June day in Munich, yet not hot—beautiful Bavarian weather that was very much welcome by my Mutti and Vati (German for Mommy and Daddy) after such a cold and blustery winter.

Mutti tightly braided my long, black hair and dressed me in the dirndl that my Opa (grandfather) Rath bought me for my fourth birthday in May. A dirndl is the well-known traditional German dress with an apron. I remember being so proud of my blue dirndl and white apron, which happened to be the official colors of Bavaria, and of my shiny black patent leather shoes and white socks.

To show off my wonderful dress, I asked Mutti and her friend Louise, who happened to be at our house visiting at the moment, to take me for a walk. We strolled the neighborhood, me in my wonderful dress that besides being in the colors of Bavaria also matched the sky and puff-ball clouds. Eventually, after turning a corner Mutti noticed a large crowd gathered a few blocks away. Mutti and Louise decided to find out the reason the people were crowding the curbs, and when we approached we took our place at the back of the throng. As you would know, I was much too short to see anything happening on the street with the barrier of adults in front of me. Always curious, a trait that has stayed with me my entire life, I had to investigate. I released Mutti's hand and before she could stop me I darted into the crowd and quickly started wending my way around the legs of onlookers until I came to the front and stood on the edge of the curb next to a large man in a brown uniform. He was holding a bouquet of flowers. I also remember the brightly colored armband he wore on his left upper arm. It was bright red with a white circle. Inside the circle was a twisted black cross. At such a tender age, I didn't know what the brown uniform meant, but it wouldn't be long before I learned it was the uniform of the SA, or Nazi Stormtroopers.

"There he is! It's the Führer!" someone in the crowd shouted enthusiastically and every head turned to the left.

Two blocks down, a slow moving line of vehicles had appeared from around a corner. In the lead car—a black Mercedes convertible—a man, also dressed in a brown uniform, stood and extended his right hand out and up. The crowd cheered and retuned the salute.

I remember the large man standing next to me glancing around as if he were looking for someone. I soon found out he was looking for a lady or a girl to present the flowers to the man in the car. Not knowing what any of this meant at the time, I stretched out my arm in salute like those around me were doing. When the lead car got close to where we stood, the man standing beside me smiled at me, leaned over, and handed me the flowers. "Here, little one, give these flowers to that nice man standing in the car." Then he nudged me out into the street.

As I walked into the street, the standing man saw me and his car stopped. I walked up to the car and the standing man with a funny little mustache and blazing blue eyes leaned over and took the bouquet with one hand and patted me on the head with his other hand.

Adolf Hitler said to me, "Thank you, little girl, someday you are going to be a brave and proud German woman."

So it was in Munich, the birthplace of National Socialism, that at a tender age I became caught up in the Hitler euphoria. I would go on to earn my place as a good German. Adolf Hitler was right that day. The pat on my head by the Führer made me want to grow up to become a brave and proud German woman.

I have never forgotten his eyes that burned a hole through me. They seemed fluorescent, as if they would shine in the dark like the eyes of a wolf. And to this day, the bluest eyes I have ever seen.

Chapter 2

Family

I was blessed with a caring and loving family.

My maternal grandparents, Karl Rath and Emma Rath née Detjens (I called them Opa and Oma Rath) lived in a spacious and ultra-modern house designed and built by Opa Rath who was a highly respected civil engineer. I remember many happy days there. The Rath home had a stoker furnace before 1918 (not very common) and three bathrooms with running hot water. Oma had the help of two live-in maids and Aunt Lenchen who lived there and supervised the household chores. Opa's office, his den, and Oma's parlor were on the first floor. At the end of a long hall was a small alcove where Opa's hunting dog, Artus, had a small couch from where he kept keen vigil over the activities of the house. I respected Artus greatly as he was much bigger than me and growled if I displeased him. I never figured out how Artus knew when I was about to do something a little girl shouldn't do, but he always warned me with his growl. At other times he protected me and never allowed a stranger to touch me.

A spiraling staircase led to the second floor. Three bedrooms (two with balconies) and two baths were on that floor. The third floor was part attic with bedrooms for the maids.

On the ground level were the kitchen and dining rooms, a walkout basement, the furnace room and laundry room with a large water boiler and scrub tables.

Opa Rath was a tall, stout man with a light complexion and blond hair. After office hours he enjoyed retreating to his den where he would smoke one of his long, ornate Meerschaum pipes. His hobby was hunting and his den walls were decorated with many deer antlers of various sizes, stuffed deer heads, and a few stuffed birds. A stuffed badger that Opa and Artus had bagged sat in a corner. Since the badger had a permanent place in Opa's den, and Artus was allowed only occasional access to the inner sanctum, the dog avoided the badger and treated it with contempt.

According to my father's account, he had the greatest admiration and respect for his father-in-law. He said Opa Rath was the wisest, yet most humble man he ever encountered. Karl Rath's grown children respected their father and his wishes; the maids feared him; and Oma outdid herself to please him. He loved good food. Before her marriage, Oma spent two years in a finishing school where she learned to cook. In turn, when their two daughters finished high school they were sent to a two-year college for women, run by Protestant sisters, where they learned the secrets of keeping a perfect house, decorating and cooking. Both had a degree in homemaking.

Oma thought idle time was wasted time, even for a little girl. She thought age four was old enough to learn to knit. Oma also knew I had been wanting and wishing for a little ring, so she bought a pretty little girl's ring with a small red stone, packed it into a small ring box and wrapped many yards of knitting yarn into a ball around it. I learned to knit when I was four years old because I wanted to get to that ring!

Until I was five years old I was the only grandchild in the Rath family. We lived in an apartment across the street, so most of my time was spent playing in the big house or the even bigger yard. Amid the playing, these wise adults taught me the finer etiquette of behavior, the use of clean language, and I learned early on that there was a wide distinction between a woman and a lady.

Radios began to be more common in homes about this time. Opa purchased a crystal set, which was placed in the middle of the table in Oma's parlor and family members would gather with headphones covering their ears. I sat on the floor under the table wondering what all the fuss was about.

The spring after my brief encounter with the Führer my parents and I moved to Lochham, a small town about five miles from Opa and Oma Rath's house in Pasing. Nowadays, both Pasing and Lochham would be called *suburbs* of Munich. We didn't let the distance stop frequent trips to the big Rath house in Pasing. Mutti (mom) and I many times took the train or, after I got my first bicycle, rode our bikes to the big house.

As Opa and Oma Rath were my maternal grandparents, of course that made my mother their daughter. Mutti was born Thea Pauline

Rath in Nürnberg in 1905. My father, Konrad Johann Dorsch, was born in 1900 in Munich.

My Music

My Opa and Oma Dorsch (my father's parents) also lived near Munich but farther away from us than the Rath's. One summer, Opa Dorsch detected I might have a penchant for music. Opa was quite an accomplished musician. He played the piano and violin, and even the zither for Bavarian dances. In his home was an exquisite, highly polished Bechstein piano. These pianos were very expensive then as they are now. Opa would let me bang away until one day he decided to teach me a few notes. I picked this up immediately and, to his amazement, began playing simple arrangements at the age of five.

"She has music inside of her, Thea," he told my mother one day. "She's not here enough to learn piano. I will buy her an accordion she can take home."

I attacked the accordion with great fervor and mastered it in less than a year. When I was blue, it picked me up. Later, I would play my accordion in the bomb shelters to calm those around me as things exploded in the streets above us. I still play today. Throughout my life, my music has delivered me from many doldrums.

Chapter 3

Schooling for the Führer

I remember how much I looked forward to my first day of school in the fall of 1936. I was six years old. As an only child, I had few playmates so for my first day I was determined to get everything perfect. My parents had elected not to send me to Kindergarten so I started in first grade at the Volksschule Gräfelfing not far from where we lived in a two apartment home. Our apartment was upstairs.

Wearing my new black school shoes and a dark blue wool skirt and a white blouse, I put on my neatly arranged backpack and made sure I did not forget my cone of treats. Every student was supposed to bring crayons, a pencil, and treats on the first day of school to share with the class. We brought everything in a large paper cone shaped like an ice cream cone only about two feet long. My father had a good job with the government so we could afford nice treats: small candies and chocolate. When I got to school I saw some of the poorer students had brought no treats, or treats that no one wanted. Their families could not afford the good treats. They looked sad, which made me sad. This was not right, it seemed to me. If everyone couldn't afford to bring treats, then no one should bring them. One of the boys who had brought no treats stood out among all the others. He wore two different types of shoes, both with holes, and ragged clothes. I handed him half of my treats so he would have something to share.

When I entered my classroom for the first time the dominate décor of the room centered around two objects—a swastika flag hanging limp on a pole in the corner and a large portrait of Adolf Hitler on the wall next to the blackboard where we students could not avoid gazing at it constantly throughout the day.

Our very first lesson, demanded by law, concerned the proper way to give the Hitler salute, which we were instructed to extend to the Führer's portrait each time we entered or left the room. As students, we were also to use the salute to greet each other whether it was in the hallway or on the playground. As you can imagine, all this led to many outstretched arms and "Heil Hitler's" during the course of a school day.

However, my debut into the world of education would be memorable but hardly auspicious. On the second day of class, some of the students seemed far under the weather and on the third day it was determined there was an outbreak of measles. I was one who caught the measles at school. All classes were suspended for a month. This nearly broke my heart; I so looked forward to school and meeting other children my age. But when the month-long hiatus ended I was back on track and thus began my education in the Third Reich—an education that wouldn't end until late in the war when my high school was reduced to rubble by the American Flying Fortresses.

My first grade teacher's name was Fräulein Centa Lindermaier. She was a devote Catholic, and for some reason she liked me. This must have been obvious to my classmates, some of whom began needling me about being the teacher's pet. One of the mean little boys kicked me and scuffed my immaculate white socks. Boy was I mad! So I found myself wishing I would be spared Fräulein Lindermaier's extra attention. Yet I could never criticize Fräulein Lindermaier. She was an excellent teacher and a kind, delightful person. After I became an adult, I had a chance meeting with her after the war. It was all those years later that she told me why I was among her favorite students. On that first day of school, she saw me sneaking the poor boy half of my treats so he would have something to share with the others. She gave me a small Catholic medallion that I wore for years. We developed a friendship that lasted until she died in 1988.

Learning English

Several foreign languages were taught in German public schools. English was but one of those languages. My parents thought it important that I be well versed in as many languages as possible and always prodded me to work hard in these classes.

Much later, after the war started, a chance arose for my parents to further my proficiency in one of the languages—English. They wasted no time taking advantage of the opportunity.

A lady from Scotland had married a German before the war and they made their home in Lochham, very near our latest home in Gräfelfing. When the war started the husband shipped off with the Kriegsmarine (German navy). The Scottish wife attempted to return to her family home in Edinburgh to wait out the war, but the German government would have none of that. This amounted to her being stranded in Germany without a husband on hand as the war raged.

Her maiden name was Eileen MacDonald. After she married her German husband, she became Eileen MacDonald Keinath.

To supplement her income while her husband was away, Frau Keinath decided to take on tutoring local students trying to improve their English. My parents signed me up immediately.

After four years of tutoring by Eileen MacDonald Keinath, I spoke English well enough that I could get by in basic conversation. But I had developed one of the strangest accents you can imagine: half German and half Scottish brogue.

A Vacation to Remember

Vati enjoyed hiking in the mountains, so our annual vacations normally focused on a trip to the Bavarian or Austrian Alps.

In 1938, Vati decided we would head off to Austria, find a hotel in Salzburg, and spend our days hiking and picnicking in the Austrian Alps. This would be a most memorable vacation because early one morning while we were still in our hotel, the German Wehrmacht rolled into town. I watched the beginning of the Anschluss of Austria from our hotel window.

Mutti was worried that we might suffer some backlash from the Austrians, but Vati assured her we had nothing to worry about as he was a Party Member in good standing and our Army would never stand for any mistreatment of Germans. And in fact, as I watched from our third floor window, it seemed that the Austrians couldn't have been happier about being annexed by the Fatherland. I saw local citizens stream out onto the street curbs amidst much cheering, waving, and Hitler saluting as the tanks, half-tracks, and trucks full of soldiers drove by.

Vati was right. Not only did we not suffer any hard feelings from the Austrians, some even thanked my father as if he had something to do with Austria now being part of greater Germany. Nevertheless, Vati decided we would cut our vacation short that year and we returned to Munich on the next available train.

Chapter 4

Uncle Wernher

My early years of schooling marched by like Stormtroopers on Party Day. In 1943 the war raged and I was in my eighth year of school. It was during this year that I had an encounter with another great man although I wouldn't realize who he was until later.

That year, my grades in my math, algebra and geometry classes were fine. When I needed help, Vati, who made his living with numbers, was there to guide me and help me with my homework. Physics, however, was not sinking into this 13-year-old girl's head.

Vati told me if I ever needed help with my Physics I could ask his former school friend, Herr Gramshorn, who lived in a big house three blocks away. I knew this family, having met them through Vati.

This particular assignment threw me, especially after several nightly ups and downs in the bomb shelter. Vati was out of town, so one night, after dinner, I reluctantly trudged over to the Gramshorns and was somewhat surprised to see a black car with SS license plates sitting in their driveway. An SS Scharführer (equivalent to an American sergeant) stood outside the car smoking a cigarette. I took him to be the driver.

I rang the bell and was let in by Frau Gramshorn.

"Ilse, welcome, what can I do for you?"

"I'm sorry to bother you, Frau Gramshorn, but I have a miserable homework assignment in physics and I thought with Herr Gramshorn's knowledge in that area he might be able to help me."

"I'm sorry; my husband is late getting home this evening. He missed his train and will be about two hours late. But wait a minute, my husband's friend stopped in and is also waiting for him to get home. I have a strong feeling he can be of help to you."

Frau Gramshorn called her seven-year-old daughter and said, "Call Uncle Wernher and tell him a young lady has need of his wisdom."

By this time I was wishing I would have stayed home. What would some old man know about physics homework, or even have heard of a hydrostatic press formula?

She asked me to sit down in the den and wait a few minutes.

Shortly, a handsome man, perhaps in his early or mid-thirties, walked into the room. He reached out to shake my hand.

"My name is Wernher. Frau Gramshorn tells me you are stumped by your physics homework. I don't know if I'm smart enough to help you, but I'm willing to give it a try. Let me see what they have given you that tortures a pretty girl's head."

I showed him my assignment, still wishing to be someplace else. But I quickly listened up when he asked to borrow my pencil and began scribbling numbers on a piece of paper. Then he drew with a few strokes a picture of a hydrostatic press and showed me what the question was about and added an easy-to-understand formula for it.

When finished, he looked over my school book and said, "The formula in this book is much too complicated. They make something difficult out of something simple. Use the formula I gave you and you'll solve the problem easily."

And I did. I now understood the problem and used *Uncle Wernher's* formula to solve the puzzle. I grabbed up my book and supplies, thanked him, and headed to the door to leave.

"You might become a scientist yet," he called after me and chuckled.

I did not know who Uncle Wernher was until later in the war when a neighbor told Mutti that Wernher von Braun visits Herr Gramshorn occasionally. It seems they were old chums since their university days. The neighbor said she had seen him on a newsreel and that he was the inventor of the V-2 Vengeance rockets that rained down on London.

[Note: Wernher von Braun indeed headed up the German Vengeance rocket program in WWII. After the war, he was brought to the United States and in the 1950s was assigned to NASA where he is credited with inventing the Saturn rockets that took Americans to the moon.]

Chapter 5

The Death's Head Visits My School

By late 1943/early '44, Allied bombings increased greatly on cities all over Germany. Especially hard hit were the industrial areas of the northwest regions. Parents in those districts were urged to allow their school-age children to be moved to other parts of Germany. Smaller towns in Bavaria were preferred as they were deemed safer. An exchange program was instituted between Bavarian parents willing to take in one or more children from the hard-hit areas. At the start of the 43/44 school year, our class gained six new students who had been shipped down from Essen or Cologne. The following year, ten more were added from Berlin. We didn't shun them as strangers; we were all Germans, after all. But they had the odd northern accents and we didn't know much about them (I'm sure they considered our Bavarian accents equally as odd).

Despite Dr. Goebbels' propaganda that the war was going Germany's way, it was apparent to most that we were getting weaker and suffering many losses on both the Eastern and the Western fronts. We were losing territory. That summer before my 1944/45 school year began, we had been forced out of Paris; most of Italy was now in the hands of the Allies, and the Soviets had pushed us out of much of the territories we had liberated in the East. (The official word Dr. Goebbels used to denote lands we had overrun early in the war was 'liberated' not 'conquered'). But even Dr. Goebbels could not put an optimistic spin on the growing number of families who were losing sons, husbands and fathers to the lists of casualties or prisoners of war.

It was at this time that one day at school we received a visit from the Totenkopf-SS. Many people do not realize this today, but the SS had several vastly different divisions. Most of the Waffen-SS were no more than elite fighting soldiers, not unlike British commandos or U.S. Army Rangers. Some, like the Liebstandarte-SS, served as body guards to the Führer and committed no atrocities. But it was the Totenkopf that would forever link all of the SS with wickedness. The word

'Totenkopf' translates to 'Death's Head' and the members of this division of the SS were easily recognizable because of the skull and crossbones emblem on the front of their caps. I would learn after the war that it was the Totenkopf-SS who were responsible for most of the horrors that took place in the concentration camps.

These men of the Death's Head came to our school as recruiters and gave speeches urging any young men 17 or older to not wait around to be drafted, but to sign up voluntarily now, ahead of time. They told the boys that they would be doing a special good deed for the Führer and the Fatherland, and get to choose their duty assignments. Plus, they could join up right now in class and not have to report to a recruiting office.

About a dozen of the boys signed up right then. The ones who didn't were scoffed at and belittled. The volunteers got up, waved at us, and left with the Totenkopf. One boy told his girlfriend, "I'll see you soon."

At first, no one thought much about it but the boys would never be seen again. And among the northern boys, not even their parents would hear from them again. Communications with the northern part of Germany was difficult and sometimes impossible due to the cut telephone wires. Mail often burned up in bombed train cars before it ever reached its destination.

These boys just simply disappeared.

My school was destroyed by bombs and I was channeled to another school where I soon forgot about the incident—we took the Totenkopf at its word that the boys would be taken care of properly.

Thirty years later, during a trip back to Munich, I ran into an old friend who told me her brother had been recruited at school late in the war much like that day at my school. They never saw him again and never learned of his fate. What the Totenkopf did with these boys was send them immediately to the Russian Front with practically no training, where they became little more than cannon fodder for Russian artillery.

Chapter 6

Hitler Youth

After the annexation of Austria and Czechoslovakia and quick conquering of Poland (events that took place in 1938 and 39), German troops occupied Norway that next spring, and then the war with the Low Countries and France began.

These later events took place in 1940 when I turned ten years old. Now it became time for my mandatory participation in the Jungmädelbund (Young Girls League), a branch of the Hitler Youth for girls ages 10 to 14. In 1936, a law was passed making membership in the Hitler Youth mandatory for German boys and girls. Yet, at least for girls, it was a law rarely enforced and a girl or her family seldom received a penalty for not joining. But all that changed with the outbreak of war in 1939 when penalties for not participating were stiffened and enforced.

The threat of penalties was not needed in my case. I counted the days until my tenth birthday and when May 4th arrived I rushed down to join. I had heard glamorous reports from some of the older girls in school of day field trips, fun marching and singing, and even overnight camping trips. Before the days of the Hitler Youth, it was unheard of in Germany for a young girl to go camping without the supervision of her parents. And uniforms! I was so excited.

An important thing to note is when I joined the Jungmädelbund. Again, it was in early May of 1940. We were in the midst of what was being called the 'Phony War' when for eight months after Poland little happened other than the quick capitulation of Denmark and the takeover of Norway. We didn't invade the Low Countries and France until after my birthday. The Luftwaffe (German Air Force) ruled the skies. Bombings of my home town of Munich were something no one thought would ever be even remotely possible. In 1940, our national pride was high and we all thought the war would soon be over.

Troop transports with waving and singing German soldiers passed through our railroad station several times a day. Great expectations were promoted in the Reich's official newspaper, the *Völkischer Beobachter.* Over the radio we heard inspiring nationalistic songs, stirring propaganda, and rousing marching music with many "Heil Hitler's" sprinkled between. Germany was going to win the war and cleanse the world of all the bad people. The new Thousand Year Reich had begun.

So off I went to join the Hitler Youth. I proved to their satisfaction that I had no Jewish or Slav blood so I was accepted. I wanted to be a good and brave German, like the Führer himself had predicted for me. In fact, as one who had presented flowers to the Führer, I went into the Hitler Youth as somewhat of a celebrity, and I think that my personal encounter with Adolf Hitler was a significant reason I rose quickly in the ranks. By the time I was in the BDM—Bund Deutscher Mädel (League of German Girls for females ages 14 and up)—I was the flag bearer and leader of the group. Leader was a position normally held by women in their early twenties, many with university educations. I was tall for my age, the supervisors thought I had leadership qualities, and, of course, the fact that I had had personal interaction with our beloved Führer didn't hurt, even if it was for the briefest of moments. But before the BDM there was for me the Jungmädelbund for girls ages 10 to 14.

In the Jungmädelbund, our activities included marching and calisthenics. I enjoyed both—we must have strong bodies to serve the Fatherland. Singing was important. The songs were quite stirring. At the time, I didn't realize they were nationalistic propaganda. I knew only that they were fun and easy to sing and I was on a grand adventure with my friends. We dabbled with arts and crafts and rushed home to tell our parents our activities of that day. My only stressful moment in those early years came upon me when I first joined. I could not acquire the official brown leather string that served as a knot for my black necktie. This caused me considerable anguish. *How could I report to my unit without a perfect uniform?* Finally I found out a girlfriend had two of the Bolo tie strings and she was good enough to give me one. Disaster was averted.

Later, after the war had turned its tide against us, our BDM duties would take on much less sparkling obligations than marching, singing around campfires, and learning how to sew. After the bombs started raining down on us, we would spend many hours and days on our hands and knees sorting through rooms of rotten potatoes to find one hiding in the pile that was fit to eat by a starving population. We would help in hospitals where we saw the handiwork of Allied bombs on the shattered bodies of old men, pregnant women, and small children. I promised myself I would always hate Americans.

But there was one time the American bombs actually saved me and my girls from an ugly fate.

It was the summer of 1944. I was now in the BDM, the full-fledged arm of the Hitler Youth for girls. At one large Hitler Youth rally I had taken the blood oath, where we pricked our wrists until blood bubbled and then we crossed our wrists with one another. We vowed to sacrifice everything for the Führer and Germany if called upon to do so. Our BDM motto was "Be Faithful, Be Pure, Be German."

I had been quickly promoted to the rank of Mädelschaftsführerin— leader of a Mädelschaft, a group of about 20 girls. I got to wear the red and white group leader band with the black tie around my white uniform collar.

It was during this time, in the summer of '44, that a select group of dedicated BDM girls were given the opportunity to get out of town and spend a week away in a Hitler Youth camp in the hills of Southern Bavaria about forty miles south of Munich. I was chosen along with four other girls from my town and about twenty more girls from other areas who had distinguished themselves in the BDM. We boarded a train (the only transportation available to us) and arrived at the camp during a pouring rain.

We hurriedly put up our pup tents on the sloping hillside. Now we had shelter from the rain coming from above but the ground beneath became a flowing steam of water. Still, we managed, and the promise of play, singing, fun and food, along with a respite from air raids kept our spirits high in anticipation of the next day.

By morning the sky had cleared and the beautiful sunny day and clear mountain air caused us to relax. A camp cook was sent from a nearby town and we enjoyed good food. After two more days of singing, playing games, exercising, and enjoying our duty of being good German BDM girls we got a surprise. About 300 meters away, on the other side of the hill, a troop of young SS soldiers put up their camp. They soon disturbed our peace by always making themselves seen and whistling and hollering at us. Had they been Hitler Youth boys, our equals, we would not have minded some polite company. But they were Totenkopf-SS, acting rude, which made us quite uneasy.

And that uneasiness would soon prove justified.

The SS camp leader appeared the next afternoon and invited us, or more accurately ordered us, to join them for what he called 'Comrade German Youth Fest' later that evening.

He had spoken to the leader of one of the other BDM groups and she told him she would inform the other girls in camp and let him know a while later if they accepted his invitation. He told her, "You will come, and we will expect you."

A girl from another group said to us all, "This really will be fun! Maybe we'll have a dance and some more good food, let's go."

I answered her none too gently, "You must be a fool, or are you that dense that you haven't heard about Lebensborn? We honor our Führer, but we do not have to be mated up with an SSer to make Himmler his pure Aryan babies. I'm not going!"

Even at 14, I was well aware of the Lebensborn. Heinrich Himmler, head of the SS and Gestapo, encouraged SS to have children out of wedlock with pure Aryan girls. The babies would then be taken from the mothers and handed over to one of many Lebensborn orphanages Himmler set up around Germany to raise the children according to what he considered was the best way to raise children to become devoted National Socialists.

One of my girls agreed with me. "I'm not going either. What can we do?"

Another girl chimed in, "I'm packing up and will run away into the woods."

"That will not work," I said. "They will find you in a hurry."

"Somebody has to do something," said the girl who wanted to run. "I wish we had a telephone so I could call my parents."

We bided our time as long as we could, until the sun had set and darkness moved in. We all figured the Totenkopf would come for us any minute. Then we heard the distant rumble of engines from the American Flying Fortresses, a sound we had grown all to accustom to. The American squadron that had taken off from northern Italy flew right over us. Just after, the bomb explosions resembling lightning flashes and red fires could be seen in Munich even as far away as we were because we sat higher than the city and looked down. The thunder from the explosions took longer to reach our ears. German searchlights and anti-aircraft flak guns lit up the Munich night sky.

I knew that any SS or Wehrmacht troops on bivouac had orders to return to a city or town during a bombing if they were within distance to do so. This would be our escape. I climbed to the top of the hill and peered over. "Ja!" (Yes!) I said out loud to myself. The SS were quickly packing up. I ran back to the girls.

"They are leaving!" I told the girls.

I heard a collective sigh of relief. We had escaped our blind date with the SS.

The SS came in trucks so it wasn't long until they had left. Hoping our families were okay, we all wanted to return to Munich, but this presented us with another problem. How do we get home? We hadn't come in trucks, and after bombings many of the trains didn't run for days because of damaged tracks. We were in the forest and had no telephone connection. We were a group of young girls on our own. But after years of war we had learned some independence.

We waited until daybreak and then started walking. The camp was situated due south of Munich. The girls were from all around the Munich area. We all walked together along the railroad track for about two hours before we split up to head our different directions.

There were five of us heading in the direction of Pasing and Gräfelfing. After a while we were picked up by a farmer with a hay wagon. This allowed us to rest our weary legs for awhile. He was a kind old man; he took us to his home and his wife made us sandwiches to take with us. When we left him he told us, "You are some strong German girls and the Führer can be proud of you. We will ask God to lead you home safely."

By that time it was afternoon and we still had quite a way to go. Yet we weren't going to stop. We *had* to get home, all the while hoping we still had a home and that our families were safe. We were still near the railroad tracks yet we had seen no trains. That told us the damage in Munich had to be severe.

We had to stop and rest a few more times. Twice we stopped at farm houses and were given water and milk to drink. Bavarian people are known for their hospitality and we experienced it firsthand. As it was just starting to grow dark we finally reached familiar territory where we split up to head to our respective homes. Before we parted, we all hugged and promised to check up on one another. And then, for me, came the longest and hardest mile of the entire trek.

The closer to home I came, the more damage I saw. In the dwindling light I saw roofs totally taken off houses and entire sides of homes missing. Store windows were shattered, the glass now little pellets crunching under my feet on the sidewalks and streets. The smell of burnt and pulverized concrete lay heavy in the air.

Now it was dark and I had only one more block to go. Luckily there was a quarter-moon, which kept the night from being totally dark. My eyes were focused on trying to find our house and not on the road. I stumbled and almost fell into a deep hole. Landscaping courtesy of the Americans had left a crater in the road that was impossible to walk around. I had to backtrack around the block. After my exhausting Odyssey I finally stood in front of my home. It had suffered some roof damage, several broken windows, and a few large cracks in the stucco walls from the bomb's concussion.

Then I felt four strong arms grab me and heard my dear parents cry out: "Ilselein, Ilselein, Du bist am Leben und Du bist wieder da!"

Yes, I was alive and home again.

When I told my father about the SS, he was livid. I had never seen him that angry. "The Totenkopf are all swines!" he shouted.

I think that was the first awakening my father had about the Party; there would be more awakenings to come for all of us.

Chapter 7

The Jews

I have mentioned the towns of Pasing, Lochham, and Gräfelfing as places where I grew up. All three communities are now considered part of Munich proper; suburbs they would be called today. Back then, during the days of the Third Reich, we thought of them as separate little towns. Both are located west of the Munich city center and directly south of the town of Dachau, only seven or eight miles away as the crow flies.

And now to the question asked of all Germans who lived under the Third Reich.

How much did you know about what was happening during the war to the Jews in the concentration camps?

It is a question that has been asked since the end of the war of all of us who lived under Hitler's regime. Many magazine articles, research papers, and books have been written attempting to answer that question. You can find among any of the three various points of view from the average German did not know, to some of them knew, to all of us had to know.

I can speak only for myself.

I knew little about Jews during my tender years growing up in the mid-1930s. I had no Jewish classmates in my school. A pair of Jewish sisters lived in my neighborhood, but having had very little contact with them, I grew up knowing nothing of the Jews personally. After Kristtalnacht in 1938 the family disappeared and we never saw them again. I want with all my heart to believe they made it out of Germany (at that point it was hard but not impossible for Jews to still leave Germany).

So my knowledge of Jewish people, what little of it there was, was second or third hand. Of course we all heard some people occasionally talk badly of them, but this was not all that common, at least in my circles. Most of the anti-Semitic propaganda about the Jews that reached my ears poured out of our family radio in our parlor.

I remember one incident when I was seven years old. My father had taken me to visit my Opa and Oma Dorsch (his parents). Opa was a coin collector and had an impressive collection of 19th century coins which he enjoyed showing me. Upon viewing one coin, I asked Opa who was the man whose image was engraved on the coin. Oma sat nearby.

"He was not a nice man," Oma interjected. "He was a king who unfairly took money from the people."

Instead of asking the obvious question of why the government would choose to honor such a man with a coin, I blurted out. "Oh, a Jew."

Oma looked shocked. "Where did you hear such talk, Ilselein?" (The 'lein' denoting their pet name for me, meaning 'little Ilse.')

I shrugged. She looked at my grandfather but nothing more was said. I wouldn't find out until years later that my grandmother's best lady friend was Jewish.

For me, the extent of the Nazi's hatred of the Jews didn't hit me fully until the night of November 9th, 1938. Kristallnacht, literally "Crystal Night" or commonly referred to as the "Night of Broken Glass" when synagogues all over Germany were burned or vandalized along with hundreds of Jewish-owned businesses and stores. Many Jews were killed, or, I would learn later, disappeared into concentration camps. We saw the photos in the newspapers and heard from the radio the reasons that led to Kristallnacht. It was the Jews' fault; they had brought it on themselves. On November 7th a German embassy official in Paris was murdered by a Polish Jew. Our radio told us that this outrage was the last straw for many Germans, and the citizens who took to the streets did so with understandable indignation. After the war, we would learn this was not the case. The government had used the killing of the official to unleash the Gestapo and Sturmabteilung on the Jews. The Sturmabteilung, or SA, was known best to those outside Germany as the Stormtroopers, or Brown Shirts. Most of us thought this was an unfortunate riot, a mindless response to a German official's murder that would not happen again. Some ordinary German citizens joined in the vandalism, this cannot be denied, but history has brought to light that this heartrending part of

Germany history was not a spontaneous reaction by average German citizens but an event orchestrated by the government, with the SA and Gestapo responsible for the killings and arrests.

Later, after I entered the Hitler Youth, speakers would tell us more about the Jews. How they had betrayed us during the Great War. They were sexual perverts, we were told, always on the lookout for young, innocent Aryan girls. The Bible, we were told, was a collection of dirty Jewish stories. Hitler Youth meetings were held on Sunday mornings. I see now that the goal was to keep us from going to church, although, unlike what happened in some communist countries, the Nazis never went so far as to forbid its citizens from attending church. They knew that would be going too far, especially in Catholic Bavaria. In fact, Hitler was born into the Catholic faith and there are many photos one can still view today of Hitler posing in front of various Catholic churches around Bavaria, and stepping out of them with hat in hand as if he were just leaving the service. Whether he actually attended or not, I don't know. I suspect now that they were propaganda photos. Why Nazi speakers would deride the Bible to us in the Hitler Youth, and then display photos of Hitler leaving a church service is just one more of the many enigmas of the Nazi Party.

The first concentration camp was opened in 1933 in the town of Dachau, by train just thirty minutes north from where we lived in Pasing at the time. It was not built to concentrate Jews—that would come years later. In those early years of the Reich, Jews could still leave Germany of their own accord. For its first few years the concentration camp, or KZ, at Dachau was a place where certain criminals, political malcontents (mostly communists), homosexuals, and Gypsies were sent. Few prisoners died in those early years. Nearly all were kept for a time and then released when it was thought their "minds were right." In the case of the Gypsies, they would be released if they agreed to leave Germany and never come back.

So this is what I knew about Dachau until my fateful trip there late in the war.

It was the fall of 1944. I was fourteen, growing quickly, and had outgrown both my jacket and winter coat. Rationing was tight, and material to make clothes was practically impossible to purchase. My grandmother Dorsch had died; among her possessions were some heavy curtains. My mother decided we would have our seamstress, Frau Munz, fashion me a winter coat from the curtain material. But Frau Munz had moved from Gräfelfing, where we lived at that time, to the town of Dachau because her married daughter lived there. Frau Munz was getting older and with the cloth rationing could not make enough money to pay rent on her own place in Gräfelfing, so she moved in with her daughter's family.

Mother gave me the curtain material to take to Frau Munz. I had to go personally because I would have to be measured for a correct fit. This brought my father into the picture, as I would need his permission to make my solo journey by train to Dachau. I thought a trip on my own might prove to be a grand time. Being headstrong, I kept up the pressure on Vati. He finally agreed as long as I wore my Hitler Youth uniform.

"No one in their right mind will bother a BDM group leader," Vati told Mutti.

So I stood happily on the train platform with a suitcase loaded only with curtains, ready for the short journey to Dachau—just one more adventure for an adventurous and stubborn girl.

The Geheime Staatspolizei patrolled the platform, delaying boarding until passenger luggage could be checked. The Geheime Staatspolizei translates into English as the Secret State Police, better known as the Gestapo. When it came my turn, the Gestapo man in the familiar black leather trench coat and black hat looked me up and down.

"Where are you getting off, young maid?" He wore round spectacles propped up on a nose that looked as if it had been broken a long time ago but never repaired.

I was young, naïve, and a respected member of the BDM. I was a documented pure Aryan and proudly wearing my Hitler Youth uniform. In my young mind I had no reason to fear the dreaded Gestapo.

"Dachau," I told the man confidently.

A look of surprise appeared on his face. "Dachau, you say? Where are your parents?"

"I can make the trip by myself," I said defiantly. "My parents know this and trust me."

"Is that so? Why is one like you going to such a place as Dachau, and what's in your suitcase?"

"Our seamstress lives there. I have curtains in the suitcase. She's going to make me a winter coat."

The man stared at me for a moment, then smiled and waved me aboard the train. He never checked my suitcase. Looking back now, the man's words of "to a place like Dachau" might have served as a Foreshadowing if I had been old and wise enough to recognize it.

So I boarded the train and was on my way for the short ride to Dachau. When the train squealed to a stop at the Dachau platform, I stepped off and was immediately hit in my face by a putrid smell, nearly knocking me over like a Max Schmeling punch.

Again, I think it was my uniform that got me a quick pass through the Gestapo inspectors, and I began the short walk to Frau Munz's home, just three blocks from the train station. It was during the walk that I saw the two tall smoke stacks bellowing thick gray smoke. The smoke twisted slowly as it rose, like a lazy tornado. Ash was so heavy on the street that my shoes left footprints.

When I arrived at Frau Munz's home she was waiting for me in the doorway, as if she could go no farther. Ever since I had known her, Frau Munz was always impeccably dressed. She was an expert seamstress, after all, and even though she had made her clothes before the war brought rationing, she always stood out. Today she wore a perfectly fitting, long, navy blue belted dress with a brooch. Her walking cane just added to her refined look.

I was glad to see our old family friend and greeted her with "Frau Munzle!" I gave her a hug. I had grown close to her when she lived near us and often worked for my mother. The 'le' I added to her name is a Bavarian way of acknowledging a closeness.

The old lady smiled and hugged me back. "Let me take a look at you." She separated herself from me and scanned me up and down. "I see you are now a proud BDM girl," she said with little emotion.

"Yes. What is that smell, Frau Munzle?"

She hesitated, then answered. "Ilse, you don't want to know."

Now, decades later, Frau Munz's answer seems to indicate that she knew something. Perhaps those who lived close to the camps had to know something.

That is the only answer that I'm qualified to give to the never ending question of "What did the average German know about the concentration camps?"

For me, it wasn't until later that I would learn more.

The Dachau Death March

Throughout March and April of 1945, the Americans drew closer and closer to Munich. Finally, on April 29th, the U.S. Seventh Army 45th Infantry Division liberated the concentration camp at Dachau.

It was during the night two days previous to the camps liberation that I was awoken from sleep by the sounds of screams and barking dogs coming through my open window. I went to the window to see what was happening. Seeing something in the dark of night was more difficult than hearing it, but the sounds seemed to be coming from not too far away, perhaps a half mile or so.

Mutti and Vati burst into my room.

"Don't let her hear it!" said my father to my mother.

"Close your window, Ilse, and return to your bed," Mutti ordered. "There is nothing we can do."

"I want to hear," I said stubbornly. "What is happening?"

My parents did not answer because they also did not know, but it was obvious from the screams that people were suffering.

The next day, Mutti and I jumped on our bicycles for a trip to Pasing because someone told Mutti there was some food available there. We had had practically nothing to eat in three days. As we pedaled toward Pasing, we came across a ditch full of bodies. Most were wearing striped pajamas. Most were dead but not all. One man with dark, sunken eyes lying on top of the pile of bodies lifted his head and looked directly at me. He did not look frightened. It was more a look of acceptance of his fate that he had known was coming—the sad look of one who knew firsthand the terrors humans can inflict on other humans.

"Turn your head away, Ilse," Mutti said, and we quickly rode by.

We pedaled on for a short distance until I slammed on my brakes. "We have to help the man, Mutti!"

My mother knew I was right, and she stopped her bike and we started back to the man. Looking back now, I don't know what we could have done to help, but that is a question I've never had to answer. In just the few moments it took us to return, the man had died.

I know now that I was witness to the notorious Dachau Death March of April 27th, 1945, where approximately 7000 Dachau prisoners, mostly Jews, were forced by the Totenkopf-SS into a death march from the camp to Tegernsee, fifty miles to the south. This took the column directly through our area.

There are two things that Dachau burned into my mind and soul. To this day, when I think of those times, I can still smell the stench that greeted me when I stepped off the train during my visit to Frau Munz, and the eyes of the man who looked at me from the ditch. I have wished since that day that I would have stopped my bicycle immediately. Perhaps I could have comforted the man in his last moment of life. But I rode on until it was too late.

Chapter 8

Flying Fortress

In Gräfelfing we lived in a two apartment home. The front door entrance led into a foyer. The first floor apartment was occupied by the couple who owned the building. The foyer led to their door. Then to the right of their door a staircase led up to the door of the apartment on the second floor; this was our apartment. Each door, up or down, was a solid door with a doorbell and key to get in. So the house was similar to what in America is referred to as a 'duplex', only instead of the units being side by side, one was atop the other. It was a newly built, white stucco house with a red tiled roof and green shutters on each window. Our apartment had a hallway, kitchen, living room, bedroom, small extra room (mine) and a bathroom with basin, toilet, tub and heating boiler.

The downstairs foyer also had a door leading down to the cellar. Down there was the laundry room that had a boiler and tub to either boil the whites or wash the other clothes on a scrubbing table. There were three more rooms in the cellar. Each family above had use of a small room to use as they saw fit. We used our cellar room for storage. The third room was the mandatory, fortified bomb shelter. The shelter door was of massive metal and wood construction with air tight rubber gaskets and a heavy bolt. The concrete floor was padded with several layers of expensive carpets that both parties wished to keep from being destroyed by a possible bomb hit or fire. Two beds and several easy chairs, plus a big keg full of water and several shelves of emergency food (as long as we had any extra food, which wasn't for long) were also on hand. And of course, each person's personal gas mask. No electric lights, only flashlights which made the darkness and smallness of the room even more pronounced. The concussions of nearby bomb explosions felt like waves under the feet; the noise plus the feeling of air being pulled out of one's nose—I hardly have the words to describe this feeling of claustrophobia and near death.

We were given warning that enemy airplanes were heading toward Munich before the actual sirens went off. Over the radio we would hear "cuckoo, cuckoo" (just like the sound of the clock) when enemy planes were 60 miles from Munich. Then we knew the sirens would begin blaring soon after that.

Our home in Gräfelfing was not immune to the American bombs. By the grace of God we never suffered a direct hit but there were close calls. During one nighttime raid, our roof and a wall were damaged from the shock of a heavy American bomb that landed in the middle of the street, leaving a massive crater just a few houses away.

After the war, I read a book where it stated Eisenhower had ordered no bombings of concentration camps. Believe it not, this was a subject of great debate for the Allies throughout the war. Some felt a bombing of a camp or two might convince the Germans to abandon the camps. It was argued that yes, it would cost innocent lives, but how many more might it save? And after the war, many camp survivors would state publicly that they wished the camp where they were incarcerated had been bombed.

Yet, bombing of camps was not to be, and since we lived as close to Dachau as we did to the Munich city center, I think that fact might be a reason Gräfelfing escaped more severe storms of bombs raining down.

Nevertheless, as I already mentioned, we were not immune. A Dornier bomber factory sat between us and Lochham. This ensured we would not be granted a permanent pass.

As early as 1938, over a year before the war started, all home owners in Germany were encouraged to build a bomb shelter. Later, this would become the law in the large cities and areas with obvious strategic military targets—such as a Dornier aircraft factory.

Back then nearly every home had a cellar where fruits and vegetables could be kept somewhat cool. In these cellars the bomb shelters appeared. In our house, our landlord had extra I-beams installed in the cellar ceiling and two gas-tight doors—one allowed access from the cellar, the other was what I would now call an 'escape hatch' complete with a short tunnel that would allow exit into the garden. All doors had to be gas-tight as the concern was high that the British might use poison gas like they did in the First World War.

Unlike in the First War, gas was not used by either side in the Second World War. Of course, we didn't know it would not be used at the time and neither did the British. Just like the British were doing with London citizens, we were issued gas masks at school and during class taught how to properly put them over our faces. Adults picked up their gas masks and were given a demonstration on proper usage at the courthouse.

One of the weapons the Americans did use, and one many Germans feared the most, was incendiary bombs. Unlike the larger, 'regular' bombs, incendiary bombs were much smaller which allowed many more to be dropped from each bomber aircraft.

The incendiary bombs had a delayed fuse. Instead of exploding on impact, they would crash through roofs and even an entire floor before they would explode and ignite, engulfing the building and everyone inside in flames.

My Friend Liesel

Liesel lived on the other side of the Dornier aircraft factory, and closer to the factory than we did. Her mother and my parents were long time friends, having gone to school together when they were young. Liesel and I became friends later. Liesel was also in the BDM but she was four years older than me, so she was leaving the BDM about the time I entered it after my Jungmädel years.

The house Liesel and her parents lived in had no cellar; therefore no bomb shelter. During the war, when they heard the 'cuckoo' they mounted their bicycles and rode nearly two miles to the Gräfelfing school bomb shelter. Thank goodness for that early warning cuckoo for Liesel and her family.

Liesel survived the war and lives today in South Carolina. She and I are now like sisters and talk regularly on the telephone. Here in America, everyone calls her 'Lee.'

◊ ◊ ◊

My Friend Sigi

It was during my second year of high school when instruction in Latin was required. Until then, all foreign language instruction I had received was in English. Yet, it seemed I had somewhat of a knack for languages, and I progressed through my Latin classes nicely.

But my friend Sigi struggled with her Latin. What I remember about Sigi was she was kind and friendly, her outlook always bright. She was also small for her age. I can't recall ever seeing Sigi without her plaid jacket that she adored and always wore even during the warmest days of summer.

"Ilse, can you help me with my Latin?" Sigi pleaded after school one day. "I'm worried I will not pass my examinations."

I agreed and began going with Sigi to her home after school twice weekly. Sigi lived in Lochham on the other side of the Dornier factory.

One day, a day I was supposed to go to Sigi's home, I wasn't feeling myself and decided to stay home. At two o'clock that afternoon, the sirens blasted and a rare daytime raid was upon us (most bombing raids up until that point had been at night).

The next day Sigi was not at school so I rode my bicycle to her house to check on her. She must be sick. Sigi's house was gone, only rubble remained.

From a branch of a downed tree hung a small piece of plaid material. It was from Sigi's jacket. The workers had found a small, severed hand. It was Sigi's hand.

I felt guilty for being alive. I should have been there helping Sigi with her Latin and died with her.

What was protecting me? Why was I chosen? Chosen by the Stormtrooper to give flowers to the Führer, chosen for special duties in the Hitler Youth, and now chosen to live when I should be buried somewhere under the rubble with Sigi.

My hatred for the Americans was complete.

Chapter 9

Americans Come Calling

It was during the first week in May in 1945. I had turned 15 on May 4th. As the Americans amassed troops and surrounded Munich, the bombings stopped. They didn't want to accidentally bomb their own soldiers. The surrender had not yet been signed but for all intents and purposes the war was over. The gum-chewing Americans rolled into town in their Sherman tanks, half-tracks, and Jeeps. Jeeps were everywhere. How could one country make so many? The Americans had taken over the Dornier factory grounds and set up a camp there— about two miles from our house, just northwest of Gräfelfing.

Words of advice about how to deal with the Americans spread through the neighborhood. Cooperate with the Americans, we were told, and they will deal with you fairly. Resist, and things will go very badly for you.

The first American armored vehicles rolled into our small community on May 4th, my birthday. I watched from a street curb as a long line of German soldiers, now prisoners, marched by under heavy guard with hands on their heads. My heart sunk. For me this was a horrible sight to witness—my own countrymen were captives of a foreign nation. I knew then that my life as I had known it was over and a new life would replace it. It felt like the ground underneath was giving way and I had no place to run. I seldom cried. I was not one who showed a lot of emotion, but I cried as I watched my fellow countrymen march by me looking so forlorn.

And it was on my birthday that I spoke with my first American. Because our local German officials had no idea what would happen from day to day, school had been halted indefinitely and citizens were advised to stay close to home and stay out of the Americans' way. Around three o'clock that afternoon, Jeeps and trucks full of Amis (the German condensed version of 'Americans') pulled into our neighborhood and stopped. Soldiers got out and began searching homes. Some of the Amis knocked or rang doorbells, others just barged in.

At our door we heard a loud knock and the English command, "Open up!"

My father was not home. Vati was employed in the bookkeeping department of the Dresdener Bank. Mutti was scared. I was the only one who could speak any English so she told me to open the door.

Two American soldiers walked in. *Americans are in our house, and on my birthday!* I considered this our family's disgrace. I did my best to give them my iciest of stares.

The Americans did not scream at us or talk loudly. It seemed they were trying to act as gentlemen, but I knew appearances could be deceiving. The Gestapo could also act friendly right before they arrested you.

One of the American soldiers did nearly all of the talking—a dark-haired sergeant who looked to be in his late-20s or early 30s.

"Sprichst du Englisch?" he asked.

"Ja, I speak some English," I answered. "You must speak slowly."

"What are your names?" he asked, slowly.

"We are the Dorsch family," I replied.

"Are there any men in the house?"

"No." I assumed he was asking about at that particular moment.

"Do you have any guns or knives in the house?"

I knew the English word for gun but not for knives. "No guns. We are law-abiding Germans and owning a gun is illegal. What is knives?" I made some mistakes with my English grammar but at least we were communicating.

He drew a bayonet from a scabbard on his belt and showed me. Mutti, who hadn't understood any of the conversation saw the soldier draw his knife, screamed, and bolted toward me as if to protect me.

"It's okay, Mutti." I asked her to sit down because she looked as if she were about to faint.

"We have only our kitchen knives," I told him.

The G.I. sergeant told his comrade to inspect the knives so I directed him to the kitchen. He came back with a butcher knife that meant a great deal to my mother.

The sergeant looked it over and said, "I'm sorry but because of its size we'll have to take this."

"That knife my grandfather made," I said rather testily. It was a beautiful knife with a handle made from the antlers of a deer that Opa had killed during a hunt. The Ami didn't reply but he also didn't reconsider his decision to confiscate our knife. I imagine Opa's knife is now somewhere in the States in someone's collection of WWII artifacts buried in a closet alongside Iron Crosses and Nazi armbands.

"Are you Nazis?" was his next question. "By that I mean members of the Nazi Party."

My father was a Party member, but I quickly did the math and in my mind it added up to any affirmative answer would cause trouble, so again I answered just for those of us in the house at the moment— my mother and me.

"No."

He didn't ask about membership in the Hitler Youth so I didn't consider this a lie, but if it was then I could live with that to protect my family.

He looked me up and down. "You look hungry."

I shrugged. For the past three days we had eaten only one meal each day of weak potato soup that Mutti made by cutting what good part remained from mostly rotten potatoes. But I was not going to admit that to these Americans.

Finally, the two men left, smiling and saying goodbye. These Americans are strange ones, indeed. I sat down by Mutti and we held hands.

"Do we have to report somewhere?" Mutti asked.

I shook my head. "They said nothing about that."

My mother looked like the world had been lifted from her shoulders.

"But he said they might be back," I told Mutti. I probably should have spared my mother this because she interpreted it as an ominous warning, but I thought it my responsibility to tell her. I didn't tell her about my adjustment of the complete truth concerning Vati.

The Americans did return, and much sooner than we expected. That evening, two other G.I.s showed up at our door. Vati was still not home from work. One of the Amis carried a big box. In it were oranges and apples. I had not seen an orange in years. There were K-rations, bread, and coffee—real coffee, not the ersatz coffee Germans had been drinking since the war started. And American cigarettes. We would soon learn how valuable American cigarettes could be. In post-war Germany, one could buy more with American cigarettes than with German marks. And of course any box of food staples from the Americans had to include their Juicy Fruit or Beemans chewing gum. It seemed that no American soldier could function without his chewing gum.

One of the G.I.s was well over six-feet tall. He had blond hair and a jaw chiseled from granite. If he had been wearing a different uniform he could have stepped off one of Himmler's SS posters. When he saw my mother he looked taken aback. He studied her for a minute then said, "You look like my grandmother. I've seen pictures of her. She lives in Hamburg."

I translated, then Mutti replied to him, "My mother lives in Hamburg."

To my utter shock, he grabbed my mother and hugged her. *My mother in the arms of an American!* It was almost more than I could bear. Despite the kindness of the sergeant, who had obviously sent these men to deliver the food, I was not about to change my views of my country's enemy.

We would never find out if the big, blond G.I. was actually a family relation; my guess is he probably was not. There are coincidences, and then there are possible coincidences of astronomical odds. This would have been the latter, but then again, who knows?

One thing the day definitely was: a birthday I will never forget.

Chapter 10

Soap

One week after meeting my first Americans on my birthday, Mutti called me into the kitchen. The papers of total surrender had by now been signed and the war was officially over.

"Yes, Mutti," I said to her after I entered the room. Frau Leib, a neighbor lady who lived at the end of our block, sat at the kitchen table. It was about mid-morning.

"Ilse, I've been speaking with Frau Leib. She has made a deal with an American soldier at the camp to do his laundry in exchange for extra soap."

The war had made soap a distant memory. We hadn't had soap, any type of soap: hand soap, bathing soap, laundry or dish washing soap in the house for over two years. Fleas were a problem for every family. To clean our bed linens we had for the past two years wetted them down and laid them out on the green grass to let the sun bleach them. Of course this could not be done in the winter. During the cold and snowy months all we could do was rinse them with water and let them dry inside.

"I want you to take your bicycle to that American camp," Mutti said, "and find a soldier and make an agreement like that for us. Tell him all he has to do is supply enough soap for his laundry and an extra measure for us. We will do his laundry and fold it for just the soap."

"I'm not going to any American camp!" I said indignantly. "I hate Americans." I was not in the habit of refusing orders from my parents but this was out of the question.

"You *will* go and you will make that agreement," Mutti was deadly serious. "You're the only one in the family who speaks any English."

I was only 15, strong-willed and stubborn, and in my mind this was something I couldn't bear. I had sworn a blood oath and felt I would make a mockery of it if I were to collaborate with the Americans even if the fighting was over.

I resisted but all of my wailing and gnashing of teeth failed to gain me any ground with my mother. She was determined to get her soap and I doubt that the Gestapo could have stood in her way, let alone me.

So that afternoon, much to my mortification, I mounted my bicycle and was on my way to the American camp located northwest of Gräfelfing and just two miles from our home. I rode under a gray sky that matched my mood.

I don't know how many acres the camp covered but it was enormous, much too wide and long to see across. The fences were hastily strung chicken wire and not very sturdy, but with all the American soldiers patrolling the perimeter I'm sure the fence had all the help it needed. I stopped my bicycle at the edge of the trees a couple of hundred yards from the main gate. Inside I could see the Sherman tanks and numerous other vehicles including an uncountable number of the familiar American Jeeps. This was where the Dornier airplane factory was located during the war and although the site had suffered significant bomb damage, many of the buildings still stood. There were now also large American tents lined up perfectly in rows that seemed to stretch to the horizon.

It was a place of bustling activity with soldiers walking in all directions. Sedans and Jeeps came and went through the front gate, the drivers stopping to produce their papers for the guards in the guard shacks.

As I sat there looking at the camp, the sprinkles started and soon intensified to a steady spring rain. Still, I couldn't bring myself to move. I sat there looking into the camp, getting soaked to the bone. Finally, I turned my bicycle around and rode home.

I did not make up any lies to tell Mutti. I was truthful and told her I couldn't bring myself to deal with the Americans. Despite the kindness the sergeant showed us with the delivery of the food, this could never make up for bombing many parts of Munich to rubble and killing thousands, including poor, innocent Sigi.

I believe my mother understood and sympathized with my viewpoint, but in her mind it was time we moved forward. Mother was born in 1905 and this was the second world war Germany had lost during her lifetime. She knew what had to be done to survive. We now had to do business with the Americans and there was nothing anyone could do about that. Life had to go on.

Off she sent me the second day. This time I actually had intentions of trying to complete my errand for my mother's sake, but when I got to the edge of the trees the result was the same. I sat there for an extended period of time before returning home.

If you think this comical, there is more to come. The same thing happened the third day.

Finally, Mutti was totally out of patience with me and on the fourth day she grabbed me by the arm and said, "Let's go, Ilse. I'm going with you today and you're going to find a soldier and make that deal for soap, and we're not coming home until you do!"

So it wasn't long until I again sat on my bicycle looking into the camp, only this time my mother sat on her bicycle beside me.

Mutti looked over the camp briefly. "We will go to the entrance and ask one of the soldiers there if he knows if any of his comrades who would be interested in having his laundry done."

I sat there, unresponsive, so Mutti put her hand on the back of my bicycle seat and pushed me until I was rolling. She followed and we picked up speed until I barely got my bike stopped before crashing into the gate!

"Ask the first one you see, Ilse. Go now."

I knew my fate was sealed so I got off my bike and approached the barricade. A soldier came out of the guard shack and stood staring at me. "Can I help you?" he finally said. He was around six-feet tall with dark-blond hair and blue eyes.

"We have a lady in our neighborhood who is doing an American soldier's laundry in exchange for extra soap . . . and cigarettes" The cigarettes I added at the spur of the moment. I spoke English with a half German and half Scottish brogue, a fact I think amused him. Anyway, he chuckled at something.

"Do you smoke?" he asked.

"No. We can use them for barter. Deutschmarks are becoming of less value every day."

He nodded his head. "I understand. I need my clothes washed. You can wash mine if you wish."

"So you accept? We will wash and fold your laundry in trade for extra soap and cigarettes."

"How many cigarettes?"

"Sixty."

"Three packs are worth a lot of money, Fräulein."

"Two packs."

He chuckled again. "Okay. I don't smoke so I usually give my cigarettes to my buddies. I might as well use them for something. I accept your deal, and thank you. If you can come back here tomorrow about this time I'll have my laundry with me and you can take it home. Can you bring it back or should I pick it up?"

"I will bring it back."

"Tell me your name and address."

I told him and he wrote it down. I'm sure he wanted to know where his clothes were going in case I failed to return with them.

"What did he say?" Mutti asked when I returned to her.

"He is the one we will have the deal with."

"For an extra measure of soap, you made that clear?" She wanted to make sure I made the right deal.

"Yes, the soap and two packs of American cigarettes each time we do his laundry."

"What?" Mutti sounded astounded. "Two packs of cigarettes in addition to the soap, Ilse?"

I nodded. "I'm to pick up his clothes here tomorrow."

"Let's get out of here before he changes his mind," Mutti said.

◊ ◊ ◊

That night after Vati returned home from work, he tied two baskets to my bicycle—one in front of the handlebars and one behind my seat on the rear fender. We had no idea how much clothing the American would be handing over to us, but two baskets should allow plenty enough cargo space.

At dinner—a humble meal of weak cabbage soup—both Mutti and I talked happily about being able to wash our clothes and linens the next day. Vati didn't join in and we could tell something weighed on his mind. I thought perhaps he might be less than enthusiastic about the agreement I had made with the Americans but that was not it. After Mutti insisted he tell her what was wrong he finally opened up. My father was always the head of our small family, but Mutti's influence with him was great and she normally got her way.

"The Americans have come by the bank three times to question me," he said. "I am being truthful with them. I have nothing to hide, but I think things are not going well."

I had avoided telling the Americans about Vati being a member of the Party when they first came to our door. Nevertheless, they had ways to uncover the information they sought. No one can ever say the Nazis failed to keep meticulous records.

"What is going to happen, Konrad?" Mutti was now worried.

"I don't know. We will have to wait and see."

◊ ◊ ◊

The next morning Mutti planned to go with me to pick up the soldier's dirty clothes. I know she was worried I'd do another of my turnarounds, but I promised her I would bring home the laundry. So off I went on my bicycle to the American camp where I picked up the soldier's clothes along with the soap. There was very little conversation between myself and the soldier. He asked me how long it would take. I told him we would wash the clothes that afternoon and let them dry overnight and then fold them tomorrow. I would return them soon after that. He told me he would give me the cigarettes after I returned his clothes.

When Mutti opened the bag with the soap she gasped.

"Look, Ilse. There is a full box of laundry soap—enough for several washings!"

"American men must be like German men," I said. "Neither of them do their own laundry so they have no idea how much soap it takes. The Dummkopf American must think it takes an entire box." Dummkopf means 'idiot' in German.

Mutti dug deeper into the bag and pulled out two bars of bath soap. This he either added extra, or, being a man, perhaps thought bar soap was also needed to do laundry. It didn't matter to us why it was in the bag, only that it was there. From Mutti's face you'd have thought it was Christmas.

"Let's get started, Mutti," I said. "The sooner I can take his clothes back is the sooner we'll get the cigarettes."

We were going to get two packs—forty cigarettes. One could buy a loaf of bread for three cigarettes. With forty, we could eat decently for three days—perhaps some meat or fish, vegetables, maybe even some fruit if any could be found. Although rationing was severe, cigarettes could buy anything. Stores looked empty, but many store owners kept valuable foodstuffs hidden away and left shelves empty to discourage the many looters who seemed to be everywhere since the Americans opened up the prisons and camps and let everyone out—desperate people with no homes to return to have few options. Even if it's against their nature to steal, they will do so to stay alive.

As soon as we had washed the soldier's clothes, we started washing our things: clothes, bed linens, towels, everything. And that evening we all got to take a bath with soap for the first time in over two years.

The next morning, after Mutti and I folded the soldier's clothes, I immediately headed to the camp to get the cigarettes. He was at his post as he had always been, and seemed pleased with the job we had done. He handed me three packs of cigarettes instead of two.

"Our agreement is for two packs," I said. I didn't want any charity from an American.

"I know, but I don't smoke and had another pack. I probably can't give you three packs every time, but I will when I have them." He smiled. "That's originally what you asked for, isn't it?"

I nodded.

"Did I give you enough soap?"

I nodded again. I didn't feel the immediate need to tell him he gave us five times the amount needed.

"Okay, if you can come back tomorrow, I'll have some more laundry for you."

"Ja . . . I mean 'yes.'"

As soon as I returned home, Mutti and I and the cigarettes got on our bicycles and headed out on our hunt for food. It took us several hours of flashing Lucky Strike cigarettes in front of the eyes of various storekeepers, but we eventually returned home with a large carp, a loaf of Schwarzbrot (Vati's favorite bread), a few carrots and turnips, and beer. Even three pats of butter! We hadn't had butter in five years. As far as what we had become accustomed to for dinner during the war, tonight we would feast like kings!

Carp is rarely eaten in America, but Germans considered it a fine fish for eating. In fact, a traditional Christmas meal in Germany is *Weihnachtskarpfen* (Christmas carp). To Germans it's a common Christmas meal entrée much like turkey or ham is in the United States. And our wonderful carp was big enough to easily feed three!

The cost for this grand meal added up to eighteen Lucky Strikes, not even a full pack!

I returned to the American camp the next day and picked up more laundry. He again included a full box of laundry detergent and two bars of bath soap. The following day I returned his cleaned clothes and acquired the cigarettes—two packs this time.

"This will take care of me for a few days," he said.

"When should I return for more laundry?" I asked him.

"I don't know. I'll drop it off at your house when I have more."

◊ ◊ ◊

"He'll bring it here?" my mother asked when I returned home.

"That's what he said, Mutti."

"What if we're not home? What then?"

"I don't know." Then I came up with an idea. "If he doesn't come in four days I will ride to the camp."

My timeframe turned out to be pretty accurate. Three days later we were home when our American knocked on our door. In one hand he held his G.I. laundry bag (a small amount of clothes this time) and in the other arm he carried a large, cumbersome box. Mutti let him in. As usual, my father was away at work. This American laid his laundry bag on the floor and handed the box to my mother.

Inside the box were treasures beyond imagination: one orange, two bananas, four cans of SPAM, a box of powdered milk, a small bag of real coffee, Hershey chocolate bars, and several packages of Beemans chewing gum (I had never myself experienced chewing gum). Also, two more packs of cigarettes. These were not the Lucky Strikes he had been giving us; these cigarettes sported an image of a camel on the package.

For better or for worse, I think Germans are much more reserved about showing their enthusiasm than the wild, informal Americans. Mutti thanked him politely but I knew inside she had to be ready to burst. These were things that would make her husband and daughter's life better.

Mutti invited him to come upstairs to our living quarters and asked him if he would like a cup of tea.

"Yes ma'am. Thank you very much. By the way," he said to mother, "my name is Thomas Horacek but everyone calls me Gene because my middle name is Eugene. I'm a corporal in the Signal Corps."

His uniform had his last name on the breast of his jacket but I had never paid any attention to it.

"I'm Frau Dorsch," she said as I translated back to him. "My husband is Herr Konrad Dorsch. He is not here because of his duties at the Dresdener Bank where he is employed. This is our daughter, Ilse."

"Elsie," he addressed me and smiled. "Finally I know your name."

I blushed and turned away. This American couldn't even pronounce my name correctly.

"If you'll follow me to the kitchen I will prepare the tea," said Mutti.

The American and I sat at the table as Mutti prepared tea. He began talking to me. I remember thinking at the time that he should talk only to my mother and leave me alone.

"So what do you do, Elsie?" he asked me. "Do you work?"

"No, I do not work. I go to school; at least I did until you Americans shut down our schools with your bombs." I in fact did have a job during the war; it was called the BDM, but that was none of his business.

"You still go to school?" he sounded surprised, ignoring my barb about his country's military tactics. "How old are you?"

"I'm fifteen."

Now he looked even more surprised and a bit disheartened.

"Fifteen, I thought you were older than that. I feel like an old man. I'm twenty-five."

"I'm tall for my age and some people think I look older than I am."

To my relief, Mutti delivered the tea and sat down with us, ending our conversation.

He didn't stay long but before he left he told us some things about himself. He was from a state called Indiana, which immediately conjured images in my mind of a place I would never want to go. Before the war, I had seen the American westerns and I knew enough about Indians in America to want to avoid them—and a place by the name of Indiana must be swarming with the heathens! I had seen in the movies where they would steal white women and take them to their wigwams. Of course, I kept my thoughts to myself. Any comment I made would only give him reason to keep talking. This American soldier, Corporal Horacek, seemed like a decent fellow; nevertheless, my feelings toward Americans were mixed to say the least.

They were our conquerors.

Chapter 11

Losing Vati

Mutti and I shared our bounty with our neighbors. Like us, all were malnourished and lacked common, everyday necessities. We divided up our soap between neighbors until we were once again out. I was glad I hadn't told Corporal Horacek he was giving us too much soap powder. Besides dividing up the soap, we shared everything we could: the SPAM, and even the cigarettes. We bundled the cigarettes in counts of five and handed them out until they were gone. I gave the little girl next door a chocolate bar. She didn't know what it was. I told her she should eat it. She sat on our step and ate it with a look of pure bliss. She left with a chin covered with chocolate.

I think Mutti and I both felt we would be doing Corporal Horacek's laundry for a long time to come, and because of that all these items we gave away would be replaced. We would find out we were wrong, and very soon.

◊ ◊ ◊

"I think that American has eyes for you, Ilse," Mutti said the next morning. "I'm glad you told him you are only fifteen."

I'm sure I turned beet red. "Mutti! Please don't even talk about that. You know how I feel about Americans!"

She ignored me and added, "Don't tell your father, whatever you do."

I got up and stomped out of the kitchen.

Mistletoe and the Last of Corporal Horacek

We would do only two more bags of laundry for our American. And the last time he visited our home, was I in for a surprise!

He had stopped by to drop off a bag of clothes and he and Mutti had visited for a while over coffee at the kitchen table. I was there, of course, as translator. Mutti seemed to be at ease with this American from the start. It took me some time, but with each visit I became more at ease. I think because I welcomed an opportunity to practice my English I didn't mind him stopping by.

I must add that these visits, and the camaraderie that was slowly developing amongst us, was not without some risk for Corporal Horacek. So soon after the war, American enlisted men were not supposed to fraternize with Germans. They were allowed to deal with German storekeepers and any such brief, necessary interaction, but they were not supposed to fraternize. I asked him about this one day as the three of us played an American card game called rummy. He said he wasn't fraternizing; he was simply there on business. Then he smiled and placed three kings on the table.

When finished with the card game, I followed him down the stairs to the front door as I always did. Our landlady kept a sprig of mistletoe over the door year around. She considered it good luck for the house. As I was about to shut the door behind him, he stopped and turned toward me.

He pointed to the mistletoe and said, "This gives me an excuse to do something I've wanted to do ever since I met you." He pulled me to him and he kissed me on the lips! Shocked is not a strong enough word and I stood frozen. He looked at me for a moment and asked me if I had a photograph of myself I could give him. Of course I didn't. I told him the last photo of me was taken before the war. We weren't about to waste money on photographs when we were starving. He nodded then closed the door behind him.

I never told Mutti.

When I returned the laundry to the camp he was not at his guard post. I thought perhaps he was on leave or assignment so I returned home with his clothes and told Mutti. Unlike me, she worried.

The next day, another American soldier knocked on our door.

"Is this the Dorsch residence?" he asked.

"Yes," I answered. Mutti had now gotten to the door and stood behind me.

"Gene Horacek is a friend of mine and he asked me to come here and tell you he has been transferred. I can't tell you where, but he's gone and doesn't expect to return. He told me to tell you to keep his clothes and use them if you can. He also asked me to give you this."

The soldier handed me a small bag. Inside were five packs of cigarettes.

"Good bye and good luck," he said before turning and walking back to his Jeep.

In the blink of an eye we had lost 'our American.' I realized then that during his final trip to our home he must have known he was leaving and the kiss under the mistletoe meant goodbye.

◊ ◊ ◊

Not many days after Corporal Horacek said his goodbye, my father lost his job. Eisenhower shut down all the jobs that were tied in with the Nazi regime. Vati had worked as an auditor of German banks for the Reich government, so now that job was no more.

It would get worse.

Just two weeks later, two Americans in business suits showed up at our door and asked for Vati.

"Are you Herr Konrad Dorsch?" one of them asked. I was with my father and served as translator.

"Yes, I am Konrad Dorsch," Vati answered.

They showed my father their badges, and one said they were attached to some 'Special' unit the name of which was so long I can't remember it now. Plus, the man talked too fast, making my job as translator very difficult.

"You have to go with us, Herr Dorsch."

"Go with you? Why?" Vati asked after I translated.

"All that will be explained."

As quickly as that, with no further explanation, they took my father away after he donned his hat and suit jacket.

Vati did not return that night. My mother was frantic. The next day an American MP (military police) who spoke German showed up and asked us to pack some belongings for my father. He gave us no details of where or why my father had been taken other than to say he might be gone "a few days."

The few days ended up being several months. We would learn that Vati had been taken to a denazification camp run by the Americans. This was automatic. Anyone who was a Party member and worked for the Nazi government was forced to go through denazification. This was the Allies' initiative to cleanse German and Austrian society of any remnants of National Socialist ideology, whether it concerned culture, economy, judiciary, the press or politics.

So now it would be just Mutti and me trying to survive in a ruined and chaotic postwar Germany.

Chapter 12

Rosenthal china

The last time Mutti and I saw Corporal Horacek was in early July of 1945. Vati was taken away later that month. So now Mutti and I had no income from Vati and no soap and cigarette bonanza from the corporal. Vati had saved money since there was little to spend it on, but his savings were worthless as Third Reich Deutschmarks were now valueless.

I didn't want to return to the days near the end of the war when sometimes we were forced to go two or three days with little or nothing to eat because there was nothing to buy. After three days with no food, the stomach shuts down and one doesn't want food anymore; at least, that was my experience. One just keeps getting thinner and any traces of energy disappear.

A distinct memory is of Mutti setting the table with her fine Rosenthal porcelain china even if we had no food in the house. "Why do you set the table, Mutti, when we have nothing to eat?" My mother would shrug and look sad. She ended up bartering away much of her fine china to keep us from starving. I remember a long bicycle ride Mutti and I made to a grist mill far north of Munich where she used much of her china to buy two bags of flour. The trip was so long we had to occasionally stop at farmhouses and beg bread to give us enough energy to keep pedaling.

And many times during the war our water supply would become contaminated or cut off completely after a bombing raid. Local officials would hand out free beer to citizens whose water was cut off or undrinkable. It was then that beer is consumed to survive, regardless of your age or if you like beer or not. Of course, Germans are known worldwide for their love of beer. In America, some people look down on a neighbor who drinks beer. Not in Germany. Many Germans consider beer to be a food more than an alcoholic beverage. When there was no milk, mothers would put beer in their baby's bottle if they could not breastfeed the baby for whatever reason. The thinking was that at least beer contains carbohydrates and calories—something to nourish the baby. I guess I was the oddball German—I disliked the smell of beer and avoided it unless there was no water and I had to drink it to survive.

So, what would happen to us now that Vati and our American were gone?

Fortunately, by August the Americans began supplying some food items to Germans and the displaced people which included camp survivors and refugees from other countries. However, these supplies were very limited. The Americans issued a new paper money that we called 'Eisenhower Marks.' This allowed us to buy a limited amount of food on a monthly basis. Our diet certainly wasn't three squares a day, but if we watched our ration carefully we could eat one humble meal a day for the month. Although I was still hungry and thought of food from morning till night, Mutti and I were both thankful for what we got. One meal a day is certainly much better than nothing for multiple days.

Uncle Willy

He was my uncle Willy, Mutti's brother.

During the war he fought with the Heer (German Army) on the Eastern Front. His regiment made it all the way into Russia before the tide of war turned against Germany at Stalingrad. After Stalingrad, we all knew that only the luckiest German soldiers ever returned from Russia in one piece. The majority were killed, critically wounded, or captured and sent to Siberian Gulags if they were sturdy enough to get there after long marches in sub-zero cold and howling winds. Once in the Gulags, most eventually died from lack of food, disease, or being worked to death.

The war had ended over two months ago and the family had heard no news of Willy. His mother (my grandmother Rath) now lived near Hamburg. Oma Rath was originally from there and moved back to be close to her brother and sister after Opa Rath died. Oma had not heard from her son. Neither had Willy's wife and son in Nürnberg, nor his brother Karl in Wetzler or his sister Thea (Mutti) in Munich.

So we had almost given up hope for Uncle Willy. We feared the worst.

By this time we had reached another of those foodless periods. This was late July and the Eisenhower Marks would not start being distributed for another month. Mutti and I went to bed hungry every night. Then one evening came a knock on our door. We weren't expecting anyone and were somewhat wary of beggars who constantly patrolled the streets or knocked on doors asking for food or clothing. Some of these desperate people would become belligerent and even violent if you had nothing to give them, and we certainly didn't. But the knocking continued and was followed by a man's loud voice.

"Ho ho you in there! You better open up for me, because I'm coming in!'

Mutti looked at me oddly and said, "Ilse, open the door! I know that voice."

I cracked the door, peeped out, then I flung it open all the way. There was our long lost Willy, standing in the doorway with a huge grin while cradling a large canister in his arms as if it were a baby.

"I come bearing precious gifts and you don't want it or me? You are two shameful pieces of my family."

By this time Mutti had collected herself and grabbed her brother, hugging him and shedding tears of joy. I carefully rescued the canister from Willy which contained 15 pounds of sugar cookies.

Willy had been one of the lucky ones. He made it out of Russia and ended up somewhere in southern France at the end of the war where Allied regulations required the German Wehrmacht to discharge him. He hitchhiked his way back into Germany, stopping often to work to feed himself. He had worked at a shop sweeping floors, and on a farm baling hay. In another town he helped repair a bomb-damaged house. All this brought him closer and closer to home. Finally he made it to Munich where he worked for three days in a bakery. The baker, whose only business nowadays came from the occasional American who dropped in, paid Willy in cookies. Willy told us the baker owed him one more tin of cookies, which he would pick up tomorrow before returning to his wife and child in Nürnberg, just north of Munich.

What a reunion we had—drinking tea and eating cookies until long into the night. Now our family was all accounted for. We were so very lucky, luckier than the vast majority of German families. Only Vati's brother, August Dorsch, was still a POW, held by the Americans. But we knew where he was and had received letters from him telling us the Americans were releasing dozens of German POWs everyday and he expected to be released soon when his turn came around.

Mutti and I lived on sugar cookies for two weeks.

Chapter 13

Truth

July 1945

By this time most Germans had learned the truth about the atrocities that took place in the concentration camps. Eisenhower had toured Dachau and ordered photographs and film be taken. He forced Germans who lived in close proximity of the camps to tour them. Pictures began appearing in the newspapers. Of course, I didn't want to believe it. After all, the Americans were now in charge of the newspapers. I held onto my misguided belief that this was American propaganda. I would have liked to visit Frau Munz, our seamstress in Dachau, and ask her if these horrors were true but by now Frau Munz had passed away.

Yet one day in the far distant future I would learn that members of my own family had suspected the worst for the Jews. To tell this story, I have to return back to an incident that happened during the war. It must have been 1943, and I remember it was during the fall because the apples were ready to pick.

Vati and I had gone to visit his parents in Pasing—my paternal grandparents, Opa and Oma Dorsch. Oma and a neighbor shared a small apple tree so she usually had a few apples in her cellar in autumn. I was hungry and asked Oma if I could have an apple. Of course I knew she'd say yes and I started toward the cellar door before she answered.

"Wait, Ilselein!" Oma said it so loudly it startled me. It was almost a shout. "I will get it for you."

This seemed odd, as I had been in their cellar myriad times without any objections. Oma opened the cellar door and closed it tightly behind her. When she returned with my apple she double checked to make sure the door was securely closed.

I would not learn until later the reason Oma prevented me from going down into the cellar that day in 1943. Her best friend was

Jewish and Oma hid her in the cellar for nearly two years until the war ended and the woman was safe. She survived. Most of her extended family did not, dying in the gas chambers of Buchenwald or Auschwitz.

After scoffing at any of my friends who talked of the atrocities, finally I was forced to accept the truth. There was just too much evidence, too many eyewitnesses, too much documentation by the Nazis themselves. And even though Vati was gone, I knew wherever he was he would also have to come to grips with this.

I could no longer deny it. I was devastated that these things could happen in my beautiful country. I felt like my life was over. My family was not religious. Technically we were Lutheran but we seldom attended church. When we did, it all seemed so empty to me. Instead of accepting Christ, I had opened my wrist and taken the blood oath to the Führer, something not required, it was optional and I did it willingly. My belief was in the Third Reich and now I had learned that everything I had believed in was at its heart evil.

Chapter 14

The Long, Hard Winter of Despair
1945/46

The German people had suffered much during the war years because of our Führer. The 71 bombings of Munich from December of 1942 until nearly the end of the war had killed thousands and left scores without homes. Endless nights huddled for your life in a bomb shelter and seeing the horrific results one bomb can inflict on a family—a mother, father, and children who loved each other but now were no more—changes you forever. It takes away forever any childhood innocence one might have been clinging to.

Everything that aided human existence was at the least severely rationed, at the worst impossible to get at all the last two years of the war: food, material to make clothing, building materials, coal, gasoline, and even toilet paper and—as you now know—soap. We hoped things would improve after the war, and it eventually did, but it took much longer than we had hoped.

Much longer.

The first post-war winter of 1945/46 nearly put an end to my family.

◊ ◊ ◊

In the living room of our apartment was a small one-room coal heater. During the war, coal was rationed and hard to get. During the first winter after the war, we could not afford to buy coal. My father was gone and Mutti and I had no income. To buy a little coal that we saved for the coldest days and nights, Mutti sold the last of her beloved porcelain and anything else of value. What kept us from freezing that winter wasn't just the meager amount of coal we were able to buy: the fact we had the upstairs apartment played a big role. Some of the heat from the ground floor apartment would rise through the structure and help heat our apartment somewhat, at least to the point of keeping the water pipes from freezing (if not us). From there, we relied on wood.

In the kitchen was a cook stove for either coal or wood burning. During the war years, each family was allotted one tree from the large forest surrounding the County Munich area, but every family had to cut and split the tree. My father and his friend did the felling, Mutti and I the sawing of the limbs and, by and by we dragged the wood home in a hand-pulled cart. Then we stacked the wood to allow it to dry. When dry, we chopped and split the wood with an ax into burning size. The chopping most of the time was my job. The madder or angrier I was, the better I chopped. Beware of an angry teenager with an ax!

Now, with Vati gone, the wood scavenging all fell on Mutti and me. Never was the smallest twig of wood wasted. Every pine cone we came across was picked up and saved.

The bathroom was always cold. It had only cold running water. When we wanted to bathe, we had to fire up the wood burning water boiler that was connected to the bathtub.

During this winter I suffered frostbite to my toes while walking through the forest gathering twigs. My shoes had holes in them and I used rags for socks. To this day when very cold winter weather sets in, my toes begin to itch. Corporal Horacek's army pants and shirt he left behind when he never picked up his last batch of laundry kept the body warm. Seventy years later, only now can I laugh when remembering that back during that terrible winter I would find myself becoming silently angry with the American for not leaving any socks in his bag.

It took its sweet time, but finally and thankfully spring eventually reported for duty in late April. That meant Mutti and I could use the money we had to spend for coal on food. Now, we could have two meals a day. Both were humble. We never ate lunch. For breakfast we'd perhaps have some cheese and bread, or when we were very lucky a few thin slices of cold cuts or a sausage that Mutti and I would share. Dinner was usually what we Germans called a 'one pot dinner' meaning a soup or stew. With soups and stews we could make our provisions last longer. Mutti and I were very thin, but we were still alive.

It was in early February when out of the blue we finally received some word about my father. One day an American Army lieutenant showed up at our door. He spoke German so my services as a translator were not needed. He could speak to Mutti directly, but, of course, I made sure I was there to listen regardless.

He told Mutti that Vati had been moved around quite a lot over the past months but was now in a denazification camp south of Munich in Garmisch.

The lieutenant gave us good news! Vati had been declared a "reluctant Nazi" – one who joined the Party only in order to keep his job.

(An 'ardent' Nazi was one who was deemed to subscribe wholeheartedly to Nazi ideals.)

The lieutenant told my mother that although her husband could not be released until he fulfilled the minimum time period requirement, his commanding officer would allow my mother to make occasional visits.

What wonderful news!

Of course Mutti visited Vati at the first opportunity, which was about a week later. I made her tell me all about it when she returned late that evening.

"He is doing well, Ilse," said Mutti. "The Americans feed him decently and Vati has gained weight. He told me he has actually gone to work part time for the Americans handling some of their book keeping work."

"When will Vati be home, Mutti?"

"He doesn't know."

◊ ◊ ◊

Now it was April of 1946. Mutti had been allowed to visit Vati three or four times but still he had not been released. I asked Mutti to ask the Americans if I could visit Vati, and she did ask them, but no one under eighteen years of age was allowed.

At home, Mutti and I got along as best we could with our limited food and other necessities.

Then the lightning bolt came through the mail—a lightning bolt in the form of a letter from Corporal Horacek. He was now home in America.

Mt. Vernon, Indiana

April 4, 1946

Dearest Ilse,

Today we got the notice that mail service is being restored between America and Germany so at least I can write you. It sure seems a long time since that last night—we left for France early the next day. I didn't get home in time for Christmas; we ran into a lot of stormy weather and it took almost three weeks to cross the Atlantic. I was discharged from the Army and got home January 4th and went back on my old job a month later. We have had a very mild winter and an early spring.

I hope by now your father is home with your mother and you. Are you still going to school or does your school close in the spring? I think of you so much and hope you were able to get your picture taken and will send it soon. I will have to close now, so write soon, honey, and tell me all about yourself and please say hello to your mother for me.

Gene

Chapter 15

A New Bombshell

April 1946

I thought now that the war had ended we were safe from American bombshells, but I had just gotten one in a letter from that country. I had opened the envelope and read the letter as I was ironing in our living room. It's hard to explain my feelings at that precise moment. I guess the best words to describe my reaction were 'shocked' and 'bewildered.' Here was a letter from a man I barely knew! An American a world away who I hadn't heard from since he dropped out of our lives ten months ago.

I sat down the iron (forgetting to unplug it) and with the letter in hand ran outside to find Mutti. I thought she might be tending the small garden at the side of the house where during the summer months we grew what vegetables we could for our soups and stews. I found Mutti there on her hands and knees weeding the garden just as our landlady downstairs began shouting "Fire!" She had seen smoke billowing from our living room window. I sprinted back up the stairs and hurriedly unplugged the iron, picked up the smoldering clothes, ran them into the bathroom where I tossed them into the bathtub and turned on the water.

Disaster had been averted—barely.

After Mutti read the letter, she didn't say anything. She just stared at me.

Since she made no comment, I did. "Can you believe the Americans? They're all crazy! Calling me "Honey." I had no idea what honey meant, other than it was the English word for Honig—something bees manufactured.

"At least he addressed it to 'Ilse.' He can spell your name correctly even though he can't pronounce it." Mutti commented.

"What's this all about, Mutti? Does he think just because he's an American that he can have his pick of any German girl, and that all of us will run to jump in his arms?"

"I told you Corporal Horacek liked you, Ilse," Mutti finally said. "And you can't tell me you dislike him. He helped us while he was here."

"I don't dislike him, and I don't like him. I have no feeling at all for him. Your reaction is unbelievable, Mother (I only referred to Mutti as 'Mother' when I was exasperated)! What are you saying? That I should welcome this? Wait until Vati gets home and I show him this impolite letter. He'll go through the roof!"

"What's impolite about it? I think he puts it nicely that he has feelings for you."

"Ach!" I handed the letter to Mutti. "Give this to one of my unmarried cousins. Maybe one of them will want to write to him." I stomped down the stairs, out the front door, and went for a long walk.

◊ ◊ ◊

Mutti said nothing for a few days, letting things settle. Then here it came over dinner.

"Ilse, I want you to write to Corporal Horacek. Tell him you welcome his letters and suggest to him that the two of you exchange letters for a while. This way you can get to know each other better."

"I knew something like this was coming. It's not going to happen, Mutti. I've had boyfriends. I can find my own husband when and if I ever want one. Are you forgetting I'm sixteen?" I had never told Mutti about the kiss under the mistletoe. I was too embarrassed (and only 15 then).

"Exactly. That's why you should exchange letters for a while, maybe for a year. Then you will be seventeen. If he's serious, and if he's worth the effort on your part, a year should be reasonable to him."

"I don't trust him. How did he know Vati was gone? Vati wasn't taken away until after this American was gone. Maybe he had something to do with that."

"Don't be ridiculous, Ilse. He could have had nothing to do with that. That is something the Allies are doing all over Germany."

We would later learn that Corporal Horacek had kept tabs on our family while he was in France, a relatively easy thing to do for someone in the American signal corps.

"Please, Mutti, can we not talk anymore about this—ever?"

"Ilse, all you know is Hitler's Reich and the war. You know nothing about these matters between men and women. You will do this, Ilse. I'll expect to see a letter from you to this man soon, and I want to read it. I know you, Ilse. I do not want you giving that man a piece of your mind. If he writes back and accepts your request to get to know each other through letters, after that your letters will be private. I will read no more letters from you or him unless you want me to read them. Now don't forget what your mother tells you to do. I'll expect to see that letter by the end of the week, and I will mail it myself, so don't think you can destroy it after I read it."

So there it was. I had my marching orders from my mother.

◊ ◊ ◊

Mutti wouldn't get her letter by the end of the week (I called it 'Mutti's letter' because she wanted it written; I didn't). I procrastinated as long as I could just like I had done when she ordered me to go to the American camp and find a soldier for our soap agreement.

But Mutti was determined so I eventually had to start a letter to get her off my back. I remember it took me at least three weeks, maybe a full month, before I handed the finished letter to Mutti.

"This little bit of scribbling took you all this time to write?" Mutti asked after she perused the letter. It was one paragraph and less than a half-page long.

"I put in there what you told me to write. I told him we should exchange letters in order to get to know one another."

Mutti sighed in frustration, but didn't complain. She put it in her apron pocket and that was the last I saw of the letter.

Chapter 16

A Second Letter

At that time there was no airmail service available from Germany to America. Or if there was airmail, it wasn't available to average German citizens. Letters traveled by train or truck on land, and by ship at sea. This meant it took on average about three weeks for a letter to get from Germany to the United States, and vice versa.

So it was six weeks after his first letter that another letter arrived from Corporal Horacek (that's what I still called him). In this letter he expressed his happiness that his first letter had found me and that I had written him back. He asked me to please start calling him 'Gene.' He wrote of several things—mostly small talk of something happening in America or his memories of spending time with me. He also expressed his admiration for my mother and told me a few things about his mother.

With the letter came a package. Inside were edible items that would not spoil during a long trip such as tins of SPAM, three cans of something called 'pork 'n beans,' powdered milk, chocolate bars, and an entire carton of Chesterfield cigarettes. The carton held ten packs— 200 cigarettes! That many would go a long way toward helping members of our family and our neighbors.

Eliese

It was about this time that my family and I would receive more shocking news about the government we had lived under since 1933—the blow this time was truly a personal one.

The town of Hadamar was located in the American zone. The American war crimes investigators had come across information that in the late 30s, Hitler had given his go-ahead for what was being called the T-4 Program. It was a euthanasia program where people judged to be "life not worthy of life" such as the mentally handicapped or people suffering from a severe mental illness were given a "merciful death."

Many of these deaths (murders) took place at the Hadamar Psychiatric Hospital. Gassing was the normal means the Nazis used to deliver what they called "mercy" on these poor souls.

My paternal great-grandfather, Heinrich Johann Dorsch (1840-1913) had ten children, five sons and five daughters. Two daughters immigrated to America in 1892. One son also went to America. I remember being told that he was killed by some accident involving a horse. With the outset of the First World War, communication ended and my family lost track of our relatives in America.

But my great-grandfather's other children all remained in Germany. The youngest daughter, Eliese, was eight years younger than her brother who would become my paternal grandfather— George Konrad Dorsch (1872-1951).

Eliese was a beautiful child, smart and intelligent, but when she was nine years old she was bitten by a rabid dog. She survived but it left her mentally insane. After her mother's death she was committed to the psychiatric hospital in Hadamar. Eliese died in 1939 and my father received notification that she died of natural causes. As I mentioned before, the Nazis kept meticulous records. The Americans found her name on a list of people who had been euthanized.

I had been a loyal supporter of a gang of thugs who had murdered a member of my own family. I became physically sick when I heard the truth about Eliese and I had to run to the bathroom. I swore I would someday get revenge.

Chapter 17

The Hofbräuhaus

Letters and packages from Gene (I had finally decided to call him that by now) continued to arrive over the course of the next year. He had devised a way to get letters to me quicker. Mail from the States to servicemen in Europe received priority over other mail, so he sent his letters to an Army buddy he had served with who was still in the Army and still stationed in Munich. His buddy would deliver Gene's mail and packages to me at home. This cut down the three weeks it had taken his mail to reach me to half that time.

[In a striking twist of fate, this soldier friend of Gene's would eventually marry my best friend Liesel (Lee) and bring her to the States.]

In our letters, Gene asked a lot of questions. Nothing overly personal; his letters were quite gentlemanly. He asked how things were now in Germany, and he always asked me if I or my family needed anything that he could send. He asked how Mutti and I were doing and how was my father? I wrote back that my father was now home and had received his documentation clearing him of suspicion of and lingering support of National Socialism. Like anyone with a government job during the Third Reich, Vati had to join the Party to keep his job. I told Gene about the wonderful celebration we had when my Father returned home.

We had never eaten out much. Mutti was such a wonderful cook, Vati had always preferred to eat at home. But when Vati was released, we went as a family to the Hofbräuhaus. Nearly every American, or for that matter foreigners from any country who have traveled to Munich in recent times, makes sure to include the Hofbräuhaus as one of their required stops. It is the world's most famous place to drink beer and is located not far from the Marianplatz in central Munich. In the 1920s and 30s, Hitler gave numerous speeches there in the upstairs Festival Hall. During the war, Allied bombs caused some minor damage to a corner of the huge beer hall but it remained open throughout the war.

Food was still in very short supply, even for the famous Hofbräuhaus. We could only get two sausages for the table so we split them three ways between us. Two things that were plentiful were German potato salad and sauerkraut so we filled up on those. Vati was home, that was the main thing; that by itself was enough to make it an enjoyable outing. I wrote Gene all about it, and that I had paid for the meal by exchanging some of his cigarettes for extra Eisenhower Marks. "We have you to thank for our celebration" I wrote in a letter.

In other letters, Gene wrote about his hometown of Mount Vernon in Indiana where he worked in the post office. I learned that Indiana was not swarming with scalp-hunting Indians, and that weather in Mount Vernon was much different than in Bavaria.

Gene always included in his packages a newspaper from his town. I found these quite interesting. It gave me the opportunity to work on my English reading skills. Some articles in the newspaper I found shocking. There were articles that went so far as to criticize elected officials and even their president, Mr. Truman. Why would the American government allow such articles?

In some letters, Gene would include photographs of his house and town. He pestered me in every letter to send him a photo of myself. Finally, I broke down and used some cigarettes to have a photo taken that I sent him. That photograph is on the front cover of this book.

I was still sixteen years old and knew nothing of the world other than what I had experienced personally. That experience confined itself to life in the Third Reich, and a life in war. Yet, as naïve as I was at the time, even I could see where this was going. I knew Gene would suggest marriage sooner or later.

It would be much sooner than I expected.

Chapter 18

A Mental Coin Flip

It was in April of 1947 that Gene "laid his cards on the table" as the Amis say. In his letter proposing marriage, he wrote that he loved me and he was certain we could make a good life together in the United States.

He did not inflate his standing in life. He told me as a postal worker he made a decent living but was not rich, and he promised to always do everything he could to make me glad I married him, if indeed I consented to do so.

I showed the letter to Mutti.

"You knew this was coming, Ilselein. What are you going to do?"

"I don't know."

My memory of the next week is a blur. I did not write back. Instead, I walked around in a daze like a sleepwalker.

I would always love the Germany I had only heard about—the Germany before the Nazis. Then again, the only Germany I knew was the Third Reich, an aberration of history I had been totally committed to during my formative years. That commitment was now hatred. I felt betrayed after we learned the truth—the truth of the concentration camps and the truth about the murder of my great-aunt, Eliese.

Yet still I was torn. The Americans had bombed our cities and towns, killing many innocent men, women and children like my friend Sigi. That night in my room, I played my accordion as I always did when I was lonely, scared, or confused.

Finally, one day Mutti tried to snap me out of my fog.

"Ilselein, it all boils down to do you love the man? Do you?"

I remained silent for several moments before finally answering, "No. How can I love a man I met only briefly and since then have exchanged some letters?"

"Are you fond of him?"

"I really don't know, Mutti."

"We won't get your father involved until you've made your decision," said Mutti. "Keep thinking about what you want to do, but Herr Horacek deserves an answer one way or another."

"If I tell him no, his packages will stop."

This statement made my mother mad. "Do you really think I care about that? This concerns your future. Never say that to me again! I don't care about that and neither should you!"

◊ ◊ ◊

My mother kept the pressure on for me to make a decision. Although Mutti never said so directly, reading between the lines it was obvious she wanted me to accept Gene's proposal. We had little, no prospects, and Mutti knew the future of Germans my age was uncertain if not downright bleak. All these years later I realize that those were her feelings. She had my best interests at heart.

But it was for none of those reasons that I ended up accepting Gene's proposal. One night in my room I sat down and wrote Gene a two sentence letter, still quite uncertain if I was doing the right thing.

Dear Gene,
    I accept your proposal of marriage. Please tell me what I have to do.
Yours, Ilse.

What brought me to my decision? To this day I can't answer that question. My decision was like a flip of a coin—a mental coin flip if one can do such a thing.

◊ ◊ ◊

Gene could not phone me because we didn't have a phone, and telephone service around Munich was still helter skelter; in some areas it had been restored, in other areas no. Not wanting the delay of a letter, he sent me a telegram that was delivered to our house. It was long for a telegraph and had to have been expensive for him to send. In those days the cost of a telegram depended on the number of words

79

and the distance it covered. He told me how happy he was, and that he would take care of what he had to do on his end right away, and that he would send me another telegram with instructions concerning what I had to do at my end as soon as he found out. That telegram (another long one) came three days later.

The next six weeks was a whirlwind of visits to the American consulate in Munich. Everything was dictated by the Americans' War Brides Act established in December 1945. It allowed alien spouses, natural children, and legally adopted children of members of the United States Armed Forces to enter the U.S. as non-quota immigrants "if admissible." It was the 'if admissible" tag that would be my biggest obstacle. And, of course, I was not a spouse. But in 1946 the group was extended to include fiancées. It was called the "Sweetheart Act." So at least I was now eligible on paper.

For the next month and a half I underwent numerous interviews that felt more like criminal interrogations. I was sent to a hospital that was now run by the American Medical Corps on three different occasions for extensive physical examinations. I was given a psychiatric evaluation.

They knew about Vati and his membership in the Party, and I did not try to hide my past in the Hitler Youth. The Americans were so good at finding the truth one way or another; I knew if I distorted any facts or attempted to cover something up they would find out about it. At one of my interviews inside the consulate a man in a business suit identified himself as a member of a brand new American agency called the Central Intelligence Agency. He gave me a lie detector test and I had to turn over to this man Gene's letter with his marriage proposal which was never returned to me.

I told Mutti that I thought things were not going well, and I even wrote Gene a letter telling him the same. But finally, and much to my surprise, around mid-June of 1947 I received my paperwork clearing me to go to America. I was given no date and told my trip would depend on when a seat became available on one of the war bride planes.

My eyes widened. An airplane! I had wrongly assumed if I went to America I would travel by ship. I had never been on an airplane.

The only information I was given concerning a possible departure date was that the average waiting time was usually three to four months. Since my departure would not be for months, according to the Americans, I felt no need to send Gene an expensive telegram that we couldn't afford. I wrote that I would be coming to him sometime in the fall.

[Note: 100,000 war brides (including fiancées) would travel to the United States between 1946 and 1948 at which time the War Brides Act expired.]

Chapter 19

Miss Cecil

Gene had told me in a letter that he lived with his mother. Since Gene was little, his father had been a permanent patient at a U.S. Army veterans' hospital due to wounds received in WWI so his dad wasn't around. This forced Gene to look out for his mother and be the man in the family. So I knew I would also be living with his mother. I have to admit I felt uneasy about this. What if she didn't like me? What if she was one of those critical, controlling mothers-in-law (yes, we also have those in Germany). In my latest letter to Gene, I included a brief note to Gene's mother telling her I hope I would be accepted. In mid-May I received the below letter from her addressed to me and Mutti.

Mt. Vernon, Ind.   May 18, 1947

Dear Ilse and Mrs. Dorsch,

Ilse, I received your nice letter and it was kind of you to write to me. Tonight Gene is writing you.

Today has been very lonesome. We didn't have any company and I didn't even go to church this morning. The days are all lonesome for Gene when he isn't working. That will be all changed when you get over here. Do you dread the trip and do you think you will be afraid to come by plane? I believe I would rather come by plane than by way of water as I don't care for boats very much.

Mrs. Dorsch, I know just how you dread for Ilse to leave you and I feel so sorry for you and your husband having to part with your only child, but we hope and pray that she will be happy in our country and that their love for each other will make up to her the sadness of leaving her own country and her people.

Ilse, don't dread meeting me for I'm just a plain woman that loves Gene, too, so we will have that much in common to start off with. I never had a daughter so don't think of me as a grim old mother-in-law but as a friend who will be as kind to you as she knows how.

Well, I guess I better close and go to bed as I want to get up real early in the morning and wash. This warm weather makes for a lot of soiled clothes. Hoping you have good luck with all your plans and that this finds you all in good health.

I remain yours with best wishes,

Cecil Horacek

I had written nothing in my note to her that I loved Gene. I'm sure it would be natural for an American to assume this since I had accepted his marriage proposal. Nevertheless, I was relieved to get her kind letter.

Chapter 20

The Russian Zone

It was now early July of 1947. Since the Americans told me it would be sometime in the fall before I left for America, I had been spending as much time with my family as I could. I had no way of knowing if I would ever see them again. I rode my bicycle to Opa and Oma Dorsch's house often. And I wanted to see Oma Rath one last time. She now lived a long distance away, just outside Hamburg in far northern Germany near the North Sea. I would have to take a train. Mutti would go with me and we made the arrangements. There would be one significant consideration we would have to deal with; it would be a time consuming trip. A direct route was impossible. Several train bridges along the way in the American and British zones were still unusable because of bomb damage. Some bridges had been destroyed by the German army in order to slow down the Allied advance through Germany. This meant our train journey would be a zigzag route. We wouldn't find out until after we were on board and the train had left the station that our zigzag route would take us through the Russian Zone.

◊ ◊ ◊

On the day of our trip, Mutti and I got up very early (the sun had yet to rise) because our train left the Munich station at six o'clock in the morning. We packed light, each of us carrying just a satchel that we could strap over a shoulder. Vati went with us on the trolley to the station to see us off. Like Mutti and me, he had no idea our trip would take us through the Russian Zone, and if he had known I'm certain he would have demanded we not go.

During the latter part of the war, most travel within Germany was nearly impossible for average citizens. Bombings had destroyed roads and train tracks. Often, communication was severed from one town or village to the next. Although the fighting ended in May of 1945, it still was difficult to get from one part of the country to another, especially so when Germany was divided into four parts. The South, where I lived, became the American Zone. The British claimed the northwest area of Germany that included our destination of Hamburg. France took as its own the Alsace-Lorraine region and most land west of the Rhine River.

The Soviets planted themselves in a large area that included Northeastern and much of Eastern Germany. Berlin was in that sector. And like the rest of Germany, that city was now divided into four sections, one for each of the Allies. So Germany was now one big jigsaw puzzle.

What were German people who had family members in the divided sectors supposed to do?

An agreement was made between the Western Allied Forces allowing the crossing from one sector into another with a special visa. Not so with the Russians. No one from outside the Russian Zone could enter, even if a dying relative was just a few miles away across the sector border. After much haggling, the Russians finally consented to allow a train to cross into and through their territory under the strictest surveillance and thorough checks. And then, how you fared depended largely on the mood of the Russian checking your papers and conducting the search.

At the Munich station, there were a few American Army MPs walking the platforms here or there but we were allowed to board without an inspection. This amazed me. The last train ride I had taken was to Dachau to call on Frau Munz. There the platforms had swarmed with Gestapo inspectors demanding nearly everyone open their bags.

In those days trains had grand compartments if you could afford one: sofas that made into beds and some even had private toilets and baths. Mutti and I shared an economy compartment with two men and four women, four of us on each side with benches facing each other.

Our first stop was Ingolstadt, the town made famous to the British and Americans by Mary Shelley's 19th century novel, *Frankenstein*. It was in Ingolstadt that Dr. Frankenstein brought his creature to life. In Ingolstadt some passengers disembarked and some boarded the train.

Then it was on to Nürnberg for another brief stop. Our last stop before we entered the Russian Zone was in Hof, near the Czech border.

In Hof, porters walked through each car reminding travelers that the train would not stop again until Chemnitz—well inside the Russian Zone. Mutti and I were nervous. Everyone had heard how the Russians hated Germans and the stories about the atrocities the Russian soldiers inflicted on the women of Berlin when the German capital fell.

Just a few minutes after departing from Hof, we crossed into Saxony and were now in Russian-controlled territory. It angered me that the Russians were now lords of this beautiful part of Germany. Mutti and I sat on the right side of the compartment where we had a wonderful view of the Ore Mountains in the distance. Pretty, snow white clouds here and there seemed to enjoy the bright blue sky as much as we did. Cows and sheep grazed peacefully in lush, flowery meadows. All this made it hard to believe the cataclysm that was the Second World War was only two years gone by.

But in the towns and villages we would see a much different landscape. Here, the ravages of war gave testament to the destruction—burned out skeletons that used to be homes, large bomb craters here and there, and flattened buildings of different sizes where people picked through the rubble.

Around noon, we ate the small sandwiches we had brought with us and then porters made their rounds informing everyone to have their papers ready. The Russian officials would board at Chemnitz.

When the train stopped at the platform, a few people got off. Only those whose final destination was Chemnitz were allowed to disembark. Everyone else had to remain on the train. As the Russian paper-checkers made their way through the train, the elderly ladies in our compartment grew somewhat uneasy. There was a young girl in their midst and, as I have mentioned, everyone was aware of the horror stories about what happened to German women in Berlin and other cities and towns overrun by the Soviets.

The ladies convinced Mutti something should be done. They wrapped me in a shawl and tied an old scarf on my head. I was told to curl up in the corner farthest from the door and act like I was asleep.

When the door opened, two Russian policemen and their German interpreter stood there. The lady across from me handed one of the Russians my papers and said, "Don't wake her up; she hiccups all the time." Mutti later told me that the woman waved a hand over her nose as if I smelled. The Russians said something to each other, nodded, and returned everyone's papers. The door was closed and we all breathed a sigh of relief. I remained curled up and playing possum until the inspectors got off and the train pulled out of the station. Luckily, the train wouldn't stop again until it reached Münster in the British Zone.

We eventually arrived in Hamburg and enjoyed several wonderful days visiting Oma Rath. Wonderful, but bittersweet as I realized this was the last time I would ever see my grandmother.

For our trip back home, Mutti's cousin Heini found us a train ride that would only cut through the western edge of the Russian Zone for a few miles. There would be no stopping in the Russian Zone, therefore; no inspections. This was a relief, and our trip home was much less stressful.

Chapter 21

Leaving Those I Love Behind

Gene began making plans in America for my arrival sometime that fall. The people at the American consulate told me to start checking with them on a weekly basis until my turn came for a seat on one of the war bride airplanes. In those days, airplanes did not make non-stop journeys from Germany to America. At least one refueling stop would be needed. I was told the war bride planes from Germany landed in Shannon, Ireland, to refuel before beginning the flight across the Atlantic. The plane would land in New York City, and after that it was up to the husband or husband-to-be to make any further plans necessary.

Before I could have my name officially added to the passenger queue, Gene had to pay the American government for my ticket to New York, which he did right away. His plan for me after that was for me to fly to Cincinnati, Ohio, where he would pick me up. Since we did not know exact dates for any of this, Gene sent me enough American cash for me to buy my plane ticket at the New York airport for my flight to Cincinnati. Also, he included enough money so I could eat something at the New York airport and pay for a telegram letting him know I had arrived safely and the time my flight would arrive in Cincinnati. These were propeller planes back then and much slower than today's jets. If I sent the telegram as soon as I arrived in New York, Gene wrote that by the time I waited to board my plane and the time the flight took to Cincinnati, all that would give him plenty of time to make the drive from Mount Vernon to pick me up.

So, with plans in place, I settled in to enjoy my last summer with my family. However, as has happened so many times in my life, things didn't go according to plan.

After returning from our visit to Hamburg, I went to the consulate for my weekly check-in as I had been instructed. I was told a seat had opened up on the next flight and I would leave in three days!

"My fiancé is not expecting me until sometime in the autumn," I told the American official.

"I can mark your name off the list," he said, "but to get it back on you'll have to go through the entire process again."

I wasn't about to go through all that again: the mountain of forms to fill out, numerous interviews, physical exams, the endless waits outside someone's office, et al. I told the man I would be ready and he gave me a paper with the instructions for my flight that would leave from Frankfurt, and my official paperwork as a war bride to get me on the plane and through customs in New York.

The next two days were a whirlwind of saying goodbye to extended family members and friends. Packing went quickly because I had so little to take. Basically, I would be going to America with the clothes on my back and a small suitcase of miscellaneous items like combs and a change of undergarments. I would be leaving my beloved accordion behind.

"You're not going to your wedding with nothing," Mutti told me. "We are a proud family."

She packed a few pieces of her fine crystal inside my suitcase carefully wrapped in rags and my undergarments.

Calling Gene was not an option because he didn't have a phone, and even if he had, so much of the phone service in Germany was available only to the top Allied personnel. And telegrams out of Germany were screened which sometimes caused a considerable delay. I could very well get to America before the expensive telegram. I would stick to the plan and telegram Gene when I got to New York.

I took a train to Frankfurt, leaving home on July 17th, 1947. I remember it was a Thursday. When the sad day came for me to leave my family behind, Vati got up early to go to the train station with me. Mutti tried her hardest to present an optimistic front and not look sad as we left the house, but she was not that good of an actress. Anyone could see she was heartbroken.

It was before dawn that Vati and I stood on the train platform in the early morning fog embracing and saying goodbye. Vati had brought a lantern, and as the train pulled out he swung the lantern back and forth for as long as I was in view. I think it was his way of telling me I would always have a home that I could return to. I hung out the train window watching the lantern swing as long as I could until it, and my father, disappeared in the Munich fog.

Part 2

" . . . old things are passed away;
behold, all things are become new."
— II Corinthians 5:17

Chapter 22

My First Airplane Ride

After a couple of stops along the way, my train pulled into Frankfurt around ten o'clock that morning. After asking a man standing behind a train station ticket counter to give me instructions on how to get to the airport, I was told of the correct trolley to board. I arrived at the Frankfurt airport less than an hour later. My plane was scheduled to depart at three o'clock, so I had some time to wait. I made sure I found the gate for my plane first and then I sat down and waited.

Mutti had given me two hardboiled eggs for the journey. Eggs were very hard to get, and expensive. It was not a small task on her part to find the eggs. She gave them to me proudly, like a mother who was giving her daughter expensive family heirlooms. I was not hungry just yet; I would eat them on the plane.

Finally the announcement came to board. I'm not sure what type of plane it was as my only expertise with airplanes was confined to recognizing the sound of the engines of American Flying Fortresses. I learned much later that most of the war bride planes were DC-3s, so perhaps that was my type of plane.

As I stood in the midst of twenty other young women waiting to pass through the gate, we were told no food would be allowed to be taken aboard. Oh, no! I had Mutti's wonderful eggs. I cried as I had no choice but to throw the eggs away. I knew how precious they were to Mutti and how happy she was when she gave them to me. Now seven decades later, when I see a hard-boiled egg I think of Mutti and her precious eggs I had to throw away in the Frankfurt airport.

I wish I could tell you that my journey to join my fiancé in America went smoothly, but this was hardly the case. I became so airsick on the flight to Ireland the steward thought I could not continue. I was put off the plane in Shannon. Dorsch is not an uncommon surname in Germany and another girl named Dorsch was put off with me. Apparently they thought we were sisters or some other relation. She was not happy. We were told that another war bride plane, this one from Belgium, would be landing in Shannon to refuel the next day. If I thought I could continue, my new 'sister' and I could board that plane if seats were available. That, or if I thought flying was impossible for me, I could return to the European continent by boat and then take a train back to Munich—a trip that I would have to pay for.

Even if I would have had the money, I had never quit anything in my life, always seeing through to the end any commitment. This had been instilled in me from a tender age. I would not return home and cause my family embarrassment.

My reluctant sister and I slept in airport chairs. And as it came about, the next day there were a few empty seats on the Belgian war bride plane. We were both greatly relieved.

I was finally off to America. Unlike the fast jets of today that can cross the Atlantic in seven or eight hours, the propeller planes back then took much longer. I would be in the air over the ocean for more than seventeen hours. I had long ago evacuated everything from my stomach in the bathroom of the plane from Frankfurt to Shannon so I didn't have to worry about that continuing. I drank water during the flight to New York but dared not eat anything. I had many times gone without food for two and even three days at times during the war, so I guess that experience helped me now.

I was able to get a bit of sleep on the plane but only three or four hours. Nevertheless, at least some sleep helped. Much of the flight took place during the dark. Perhaps this helped as I could not see the vast ocean so far below me.

It was early morning on Saturday, July 19th, when the coast of the United States came into view. I was never so glad to see anything in my life. Maybe I would in fact make it to America without crashing and ending up in Davey Jones' Locker. It was a clear day. Besides being slower than today's jets, propeller planes back then flew at much lower altitudes. I saw the Statue of Liberty and remember being surprised to see that it was on an island. The tires squealed as we touched down in America and after a lengthy time taxiing, the plane finally came to rest and the cabin door opened. I, along with all the other girls (many of whom seemed quite frightened), descended the stairs and set foot in America.

Chapter 23

Stranded

Okay, Ilse. Compose yourself. That was my thought.

First thing was to buy my ticket to Cincinnati, then telegram Gene the details. I got this done relatively smoothly. My flight to Cincinnati would not depart until that evening. I took my ticket to the Western Union booth and sent a telegram to Mount Vernon, Indiana, giving Gene my flight number and arrival time. Gene had written in a letter that it would take him about five hours to drive to Cincinnati. My plane wouldn't leave for eight hours and then the flight was three hours long; I felt relieved that he would have plenty of time.

My hunger now caught up with me. Because I didn't want to take the chance of getting sick on the plane to New York like I had on the plane to Shannon, I hadn't eaten in two days. Not since the oatmeal Mutti prepared for me at home the morning I left Munich. I used some money Gene had sent to buy a ham and cheese sandwich and a banana at a food counter inside the airport.

I whiled away the hours: walking around (but never straying far from my gate), sitting and looking at Americans and their clothes, looking out all the windows hoping to see the Empire State Building but apparently it was too far from the airport.

At last the announcement to board for the flight to Cincinnati came over the speaker. I was glad that I had been given a window seat so I could see lights of the American cities and towns as I flew over. This flight I actually enjoyed. Perhaps I had by now graduated to a veteran flyer, or perhaps it was because my journey was almost over.

Or at least I thought.

The plane touched down in Cincinnati Saturday night. Exhaustion now overtook me. I was glad Gene would be here to end my Odyssey.

Gene was not there! All sorts of thoughts went through my mind. Had Gene changed his mind and abandoned me? What was I to do now? My ticket ended in Cincinnati. I didn't have enough money even for a bus ride to Mount Vernon. I explained my situation to the airline people. Several of them huddled behind a ticket counter and discussed my situation. I think they were quite perplexed about what to do with this young girl speaking to them with a half-German and half-Scottish accent.

"A war bride, you say? And your husband-to-be is not here to pick you up?"

"Yes."

"My goodness."

One man tried calling Mount Vernon. Since Gene didn't have a phone he tried calling the town's post office where I told him Gene worked, but it was Saturday night. No one was there.

As all this was happening, a man stood behind me whose flight to St. Louis was scheduled to leave shortly. It was obvious that he had overheard the talk of my plight.

"I will buy this young lady's ticket to wherever it is that she needs to go," he said behind me.

"There's no airline service to Mount Vernon, Indiana," said one of the men behind the counter. "There is service to Evansville, not far from there, but the next flight isn't until Monday."

"Are there any seats open on my flight to St. Louis?"

The ticket man checked. "Yes, sir."

"I'll take her with me to St. Louis and find a way to get her to Indiana by hook or by crook. If a plane isn't available, I'll get her a train or bus ticket."

I was not consulted about any of this and mostly ignored. I'm sure the airline people were just happy to get rid of me. I was an alien under bond and they could not release me to go about on my own. So like an extra piece of luggage, I boarded an airplane to St. Louis with this man.

During the flight I learned that his name was Mr. Fisher. He asked me how things were in Germany now that the war was over. Then he took some coins from a pocket.

"This is called a half dollar and that's what it's worth, half of a dollar. This is a quarter; it's worth twenty-five cents or a quarter of a dollar." He showed me and explained about a dime, a nickel, and a penny.

"I heard you tell the airline people that you were going to Mount Vernon, Indiana. Is that right?"

"Yes, it's on a river."

"I'm familiar with the area. I've done business in Evansville. It's a larger town not far from Mount Vernon. When we get to St. Louis, I will buy you a plane ticket to Evansville and give you money for a train or bus to Mount Vernon."

I was so taken aback by the kindness of this American I could muster up only a feeble "Thank you."

The flight from Cincinnati to St. Louis was not long—about two hours if memory serves. When we landed he took me to the desk of an airline that flew to Evansville. A plane left in one hour! He bought my ticket and gave me money. As I said goodbye to Mr. Fisher I asked him for his address and told him that I, or my husband if I ever found him, would someday reimburse him. He said that wasn't necessary but I insisted (I was one of the proud Dorschs) so he wrote his address on a piece of paper.

So here I was on my fifth airplane flying to a place called Evansville. Compared to the previous airplanes I had been on, this one was very small. A tall man getting on board had to stoop over to walk down the aisle. I think I counted eight seats, half of which were empty. When the propellers began turning I could hear popping noises, and in the tarmac lights saw thick black smoke belching from the engines. Thankfully, this subsided as the engines warmed up, but if this weren't enough to give one pause it now started raining. This continued and delayed our takeoff for about a half hour, but then the pilot apparently decided 'what the heck, let's go anyway' and we took off into a pouring rain.

The pilot climbed the airplane above the rain, but turbulence caused our rickety old plane to shake like a wet dog nearly all the way to Evansville. Everyone on board breathed a sigh of relief when the landing gear finally settled down on the landing strip in Evansville. It was now 2:00 a.m. on Sunday, July 20th. Getting this far had taken me three days and during that time I had had one small meal in the New York airport. If ever an example was needed for utter exhaustion, I was it.

I asked at the airline desk how I could get to Mount Vernon. "Is there a bus or a train?" They had both the bus and train schedules on hand. A bus wouldn't leave from the downtown Greyhound Station until noon, but there was a mail train going to St. Louis with a stop to drop off mail in Mount Vernon that left in an hour. They told me if I hurried, maybe I could make it.

I asked the best way to get to the train station as quickly as possible and was told a taxi was the only way I could get there in time. Thanks to Mr. Fisher, I had enough money for the taxi ride and train ticket.

I barely made it in time, but in forty-five minutes I was on my first American train, waiting to pull out of the Evansville station.

Chapter 24

20 July 1947

Mount Vernon is only about twenty miles west of Evansville, so my train ride was very brief. Apparently everyone else on the train was going to St. Louis as I was the only one who exited in Mount Vernon. If you want to count the mail, then there were two of us who got off.

So what would be my next plan now that I had finally arrived in Mount Vernon? It was very hot inside the train station so I sat down on a bench outside on the platform. It was the middle of the night; I decided I would wait until the morning and then somehow try to find Gene. I had his home address from the letters I had written him and he had told me he worked at the post office. Surely I'd be able to find him at one or the other of those places.

I had sat there for about a half hour. As tired as I was I'm surprised I didn't doze off, but the last three days had been so overwhelming. I had too much on my mind. I still didn't know why Gene had not been in Cincinnati to greet me. I was a little afraid. How would I get home if Gene had changed his mind? I was out of money and had come to America with little more than the clothes on my back. I did have Mutti's crystal. If I sold that would it be enough to get me home?

A truck drove up and stopped. The sign on the truck door read U.S. Postal Service. A man got out, stared at me briefly, and took a cart into the station. Obviously he was the one picking up the mail that got off the train with me. As he loaded the bags of mail into his truck, he glanced at me several times.

"What are you doing sitting here in the middle of the night, Missy?" he asked after he loaded the last bag.

I ignored the stranger.

"Are you waiting for someone?"

I finally said, "I'm from Germany and I'm looking for a man to marry." Of course I hadn't phrased this properly and he began laughing.

"Well, there's a few around these parts that you might find. Anyone particular?"

"His name is Gene Horacek."

He laughed again. "I know Gene; he works at the post office with me. Jump in and I'll take you to his house."

"Thank you, but I will wait until morning." I was a bit leery of this gregarious stranger.

He shrugged. "Suit yourself."

He started to get in his truck when I sprang up, grabbed my suitcase, ran to the passenger side door, opened it and got in.

"Okay, off we go," he said as he put the truck in gear.

The drive was short, no more than three or four blocks. He stopped in front of a large house.

"Stay in the truck," he instructed me. "I'll get Gene out of bed. I can't wait to see the look on his face," he chuckled.

He walked to the front door and started knocking. It took several ever louder knocks before the door finally opened. Answering the door was not Gene, but his mother.

"Miss Cecil," said my driver, "I have a package for you."

Chapter 25

The Big Sleep

Gene's mother welcomed me into the house with a big hug and then ran to wake Gene.

He came out in pajamas and robe and embraced me. If ever a man looked flabbergasted, it was Gene Horacek on that day.

"I thought you weren't coming until the fall, Elsie."

"A seat opened up on one of the war bride planes and I left Munich three days ago. I sent you a telegram yesterday from New York City."

He looked astounded. "I never received a telegram. How did you get here?"

I told him about my angel of deliverance, Mr. Fisher. He seemed quite embarrassed by what I had gone through, even though my struggles were not his fault. "I am so sorry, Elsie. First thing in the morning I'll send a telegram to your parents letting them know you arrived safe and sound."

"She has to be exhausted, Gene," his mother said then turned to me. "Let's get you to bed, my dear." Gene picked up my suitcase and followed me and his mother to a bedroom on the main floor. Gene's bedroom was upstairs. "This will be your bedroom until you and Gene marry."

"May I bathe first?" I asked. I had not bathed in three days.

"Oh, yes, of course, my dear."

After I bathed, we talked briefly but they knew I was out on my feet so they left me. I went to my room and Gene closed my door behind him. It was now five o'clock in the morning.

I slept for twenty-four hours.

Breakfast in America

I finally woke up near breakfast time a full day after I arrived in Mount Vernon. I could hear activity in the house so I knew someone was up. I had changed undergarments after my bath, but now had to put on the skirt and blouse I had been wearing for three days because it was all I had.

I went to the kitchen where I heard the activity. Gene sat at the kitchen table reading the newspaper while his mother cooked. When he saw me, Gene's eyes lit up. He threw down the newspaper, stood up, and hugged me. His mother also seemed very happy that I had finally risen from my hibernation. Perhaps they thought I had died.

Gene gave me the telegram I had sent from New York. It had arrived twelve hours ago while I was already sleeping in Mount Vernon.

Mrs. Horacek was preparing an American breakfast of scrambled eggs, bacon, and biscuits—a meal new and foreign to me. She sat a plate of butter on the table that was more butter than I had seen in seven years. And the eggs! How did the Americans get so many eggs? I remembered the two precious eggs Mutti had given me that I was forced to throw away. Gene's mother sat a plate in front of me overflowing with food.

"You are so thin, my dear. You must eat."

"Thank you, Mrs. Horacek."

"Let's have none of this 'Mrs. Horacek' business. I would like for you to call me 'Mom.' I would never try to replace your mother, but I love you like the daughter I never had."

I nodded and started eating. It was delicious and I ate as much as I could, but my lack of food for so long—the war years and the recent trip—had shrunken my stomach to a point that I couldn't eat a great deal. After she had served both me and Gene, she left the kitchen to give us some time alone together.

"This is the happiest day of my life so far, Elsie," Gene said. "It will only be replaced by the day we marry. I'd like to do that right away. What do you say? If I can get things arranged, can we marry in the next few days?" He reached over and took my hand.

"Yes, Gene."

He jumped up in excitement then sat back down.

"I haven't bought a ring yet because I thought you wouldn't be here for three or four more months. But I'll get the rings today after I get off work. I've been saving money ever since you agreed to marry me, and

I've asked my mother to take you to Evansville today to shop for clothes and other things you need. Get anything you want."

I become Elsie

I have never figured out why many Americans struggle so mightily to say 'Ilse.' Some can pronounce it but many tussle with it. I now became 'Elsie' and still to this day that's what many people call me.

◊ ◊ ◊

The production of American cars had shut down during the war when all the factories switched to making tanks, bombers, fighter aircraft, and other war matériel. In 1947, people who wanted a car had two choices: buy an old prewar jalopy, or put their name on a waiting list for a new car. Gene put his name on a waiting list for a brand new Chevrolet but it wouldn't arrive for several more months. The new car would cost what I thought was an astronomical amount—$925.

A friend of Gene's mother, a lady named Cleo, owned an old car and she drove Gene's mother and me to Evansville to shop—my first ever shopping spree. Before the day was out, we had bought things at three different dry goods stores and ate lunch at the Woolworth's diner counter where I had a sandwich and a drink called a 'cherry fizz.'

Gene's mother ('Mom') was so kind to me, as was her friend Cleo.

I was treated very kindly by the American shopkeepers, not just on this day in Evansville but on subsequent days in Mount Vernon. I learned that many people in this area of southern Indiana had German roots. I can remember only two times that my German birth caused someone to comment negatively.

Somehow the Mount Vernon newspaper had learned about me and it published an article entitled 'Munich Maid Flies to Mt. Vernon to Marry Wartime G.I. Sweetheart.' My photo was included. The day after the article appeared, Mom went shopping for a pair of shoes and took me with her to a small shoe store in Mount Vernon. The woman behind the counter recognized me from the photograph and when

Mom began to pay for her purchase the woman said, "Is this the German gal in the newspaper?"

"Why yes it is," said Mom.

The woman sneered and said, "Miss Cecil, the only reason these 'war brides' come over here is so they have something to eat and because their husbands buy them clothes."

I didn't pick up on the rudeness but Mom did. She told the woman that she would never shop there again, and she left the shoes on the counter. "Let's go, Elsie." I followed her out, still not fully understanding.

The other incident involved a woman who had lost her son on D-Day. I respected her because she had the courage to tell me her thoughts to my face. She told me about her son and that if we ever came across each other on the street in Mount Vernon she would avoid me. She told me not to take it personally, but she was not ready to interact with a German. I told her I understood this, and I did. I had had negative feelings toward Americans for years brought on by their bombing of my city and the deaths of innocent people like my friend Sigi.

Chapter 26

Morganfield and the McCurdy Hotel

Gene and I married four days after I arrived in Mount Vernon. Our anniversary is July 24. That day was on a Thursday that year (1947) exactly one week after I left my family in Munich. From the Evansville Greyhound depot we took a bus to Morganfield, Kentucky, and were married by a Justice of the Peace. The newspaper article with my picture had already been published, and although he never said so, I think Gene thought having the ceremony away from Mount Vernon was best. He wanted to avoid any incidents that could put a damper on the wedding for me.

Our rings were simple gold bands.

Our honeymoon was two nights at the McCurdy Hotel in Evansville. I had never seen such opulence: marble floors, lavish woodwork all about, a swank restaurant where we ate our wedding night dinner, and, unbelievably, a bathroom in every room!

Gene told me my wedding present was too big to bring on our honeymoon. When we got back to Mount Vernon he presented me with a brand new bicycle with a basket on the front handlebars! It was a wonderful gift.

"I know how important your bicycle was to you in Germany, Elsie."

I would eventually learn to drive, but even after I did I still rode my bicycle everywhere. I don't doubt that some Mount Vernon locals probably got a chuckle or shook their heads when the German girl with the funny Scot accent rode by with groceries in her basket.

Gene and I settled in and began our life together. He was always kind and caring, unselfish with me, and a man's man. My love for him grew.

I was now Ilse Horacek.

◊ ◊ ◊

Learning to Drive

Our new car arrived in November of that year. It was a black, four-door, 1948 Chevrolet Fleetline. Now we could go anywhere.

Gene and his uncle decided that I needed to learn to drive. Herschel Thomas (Thomas was Gene's mother's maiden name and he was her brother) was called 'Straw' by everyone in Mount Vernon because he was 6 feet and 4 inches tall and very thin.

Uncle Straw was quite the character. He owned a 1936 Ford that had long ago seen its better days so if I had a mishap it wouldn't be that big of a thing. Teaching me in that old car turned out to be a wise decision.

He took me out on a lonely gravel road far out in the country and explained how to shift the transmission using the clutch and the gearstick that rose up from the floor. He briefly went over how to steer the car and that was my lesson. It took about five minutes. Uncle Straw forgot to mention the brakes. He got out and we switched seats.

"Okay, Elsie, off you go," he said while nervously lighting a cigarette.

I took some time looking things over, then he told me to put my left foot on the clutch pedal and push it to the floor. Then my instructions were to move the gear shift to first gear. After much grinding I got the shifter in the right spot.

"Okay, Elsie, let the clutch out SLOWLY with your left foot."

I let it our much too quickly. The car jerked forward a few feet and stalled out.

"That's okay," he said. He helped me get the transmission in neutral and restart the car. "Let's try again. Just remember to let the clutch out slower this time."

This time I got the car moving without stalling and off I went, swerving from one edge of the road to the other, coughing the engine, and grinding gears all the way. Before long, the end of the road loomed ahead.

"Okay, Elsie, stop the car. I'll turn it around and you can drive back." He lit another cigarette. Looking back I hope I wasn't the cause of Uncle Straw becoming a chain smoker.

Since the brakes hadn't been mentioned, I assumed if I took my foot off the gas pedal the car would know it was supposed to stop. This car hadn't learned that lesson yet and I went crashing through the fence at the end of the road and into a farmer's field. Now the German girl was heading through a freshly tilled cornfield directly toward an American's barn, like a U-boat torpedo on its way through the water seeking an Allied ship.

"Jumpin' Jehoshaphat!" Uncle Straw screamed. "Hit the brakes, Elsie!"

Instead, I mistakenly stomped on the gas and crashed through several hay bales which failed to even slow us down. The farmer had by now come out from his barn and stood directly in my path. Wearing overalls and carrying a pitch fork, he stood frozen. At the last minute I swerved away from him as he dove out of my way and flopped on the ground. He got up and threw his pitchfork, striking and bouncing off the trunk of the car. Finally, Uncle Straw reached over and turned the ignition key, killing the engine. We drifted to a stop. The farmer, a heavyset man with red hair, ran up to my side of the car.

"What in the hell is wrong with you?" the farmer yelled. "Hey, I recognize you. I saw your picture in the newspaper. You're that German broad who married my mailman."

Uncle Straw was now outside the car and trying to explain. "I'm teaching her to drive."

"Well, you're a sorry-ass teacher! That crazy Kraut mowed down my fence!"

I took no offense to his remark. Instead it got me to giggling and I had to cover my mouth with my hand trying to stifle my laughter. The farmer thought I was crying and tried to console me.

"Don't cry, girlie. I'm sorry I called you a crazy Kraut. I can fix the fence."

So this was my comical introduction to driving in America, an episode worthy of the Three Stooges.

Believe it or not, I did eventually learn to drive.

◊ ◊ ◊

My Music Returns

One day in December, Gene drove us to Evansville to see a Christmas movie everyone was talking about. The title was *Miracle on 34th Street,* a story about a man who thought he was the real Saint Nickolas. Leaving the theater we passed a music store. In the window was an assortment of musical instruments: a trumpet, trombone, violin, a clarinet, and an accordion. I had to stop and look.

"I used to play the accordion back in Germany, Gene," I said wistfully.

Two weeks later on Christmas Day, that very accordion sat under the tree with my name on it. Gene had waited until I fell asleep, and then quietly left the bedroom and brought in the accordion from the trunk of his car and placed it under the tree.

Chapter 27

Now a Surprise for Gene

By the spring of 1948 I was content and very happy in America (and I was no longer knocking down fences).

This is truly a great country. With just a couple of exceptions the people of Mount Vernon couldn't have been kinder to me. Gene and I were happy together. My mental coin flip in Munich had landed on its lucky side.

I wrote Mutti and Vati every week and received their letters in turn. Mail moved faster by now. Instead of all the mail being transported between the continents by boat, airmail was now available. The three weeks on average it had taken a letter to get to or from Munich a year ago was now on average one week. My parents and I numbered our letters so we would know if any got lost. Gene got a telephone after I arrived, but calling my parents was not practical at that time. Those were the days of party lines when others on the same line could listen in. If I had called I would be speaking in German to my parents, which would have thwarted a nosey neighbor. The biggest stumbling block back then was a three-minute telephone call to Germany cost $20, equal to over $200 now!

◊ ◊ ◊

It was during this time (spring of '48) that I missed a period. Then the next month another.

Gene badly wanted children so I wasn't going to tell him that possibly I was pregnant. I wanted to be sure. Instead, I told his mother and she went with me to the doctor in Evansville. He confirmed my suspicions but expressed some concern because of my history of a diet severely lacking in nutrition.

That evening I told Gene. His reaction nearly scared me. He whooped and shouted like a lunatic. He said we would celebrate and then after that I was to go to bed and stay there. For a woman with a healthy pregnancy this was ridiculous; everyone knew that, even back then. I told him it would not be good for me to do that. That night after Gene fell asleep, I went to the den and played a song on my accordion for the child in my womb. I did this for all my children when I learned they were headed my way.

Looking back, perhaps I should have listened to my husband, at least in the last weeks of my term. Roger, our first child, was born on the 16th of November 1948. He was 2½ months premature, weighing only 3½ pounds. He stayed in the Deaconess Hospital incubator until the full nine month term was up at which time he weighed 5 pounds. At that time we were allowed to take him home. He turned out to be a healthy, robust boy.

Gene and I would have three more children together—none of them premature. Our children in order by birth: Roger; Danny (John Daniel) born in July 1950 at Deaconess; Connie (Constance Jean) born in December of 1951, also at Deaconess; and Maryhelen. Maryhelen was born in May of 1954 at St. Mary's Hospital in Evansville. Our former doctor had died and our new doctor was Catholic and treated all his patients at the Catholic hospital in town. We liked St. Mary's much better.

When I first found out I was expecting, I decided to wait to tell Mutti and Vati. I knew they would worry so I wanted to wait until the baby was born to tell them. Gene wrote them a letter in English while I was still in the hospital. When I got home I wrote them a long letter.

So now, the little girl who had given flowers to Adolf Hitler had a family in America.

Chapter 28

Danny

My pregnancy with Danny, our second child, was very easy and his birth was quick and painless. It was as if he refused to cause his mother pain. At birth and for the first few months he was healthy and normal in all ways. But at about eight months old he began to cry often and did not want to stand or try to walk. Then we noticed breakouts on his skin in his groin area and under his ears. Nodules started appearing in these areas. Our doctor lanced and drained them, which we were told years later was perhaps the wrong thing to do. Danny was in and out of Deaconess Hospital in Evansville and finally taken to Riley Hospital in Indianapolis.

By this time I was expecting Connie. In fact, she was born on the second floor of Deaconess while Danny was on the third floor in the isolation ward because of his infections. Nurses would roll me in a wheelchair to Danny's door so I could see him but I was told it was for Danny's welfare that I go no further. When he saw me he tried to reach his little arms out to me and cried "Mommy, Mommy." This broke my heart. I was not allowed to go to him and I felt totally helpless.

He was treated for awhile and then released to return home.

Needless to say, Gene and I had our hands full: a three-year-old boy, a newborn baby girl, and a sick two-year-old. At that time, Gene's mother was employed as a house mother at the Mooseheart Orphanage in Mooseheart, near Chicago. Gene's aunt, Uncle Straw's wife, helped when she could, and a couple of kindly neighbor ladies took Roger home with them at times. But needless to say, the load was on Gene and me (as we wanted it to be).

Then in March of 1953 we had to take Danny to Riley Hospital in Indianapolis. There they diagnosed leukemia. We were told there was nothing more they could do for Danny and that he could die at any time. I was not going to leave him among strangers so we took him home. When Gene told his mother, she decided to return to Mount Vernon.

Roger was nearly five by then and he and Danny shared a bedroom. Roger would sit on his bed across from Danny and tell him funny stories to amuse him. I still hear in my ears the laughter of that sick little boy when his big brother cheered him up. Once, a city fire truck with sirens blaring passed by the house and Danny asked Roger, "What was that?" Roger told him it was a fire whistle and then started jumping up and down while mimicking the sound of the whistle. After that, Danny would say to Roger: "Ooh, make fire issel." He wanted to laugh and be happy.

But happiness for Danny was not to be gained on this earth. As Danny's condition worsened, we moved him into another room and Gene and I took turns sleeping with him. In the early morning hours of August 12, 1953, Gene awakened me and said, "Elsie, come quickly."

I ran into Danny's bedroom. His breathing was extremely labored. His little chest made one more move then his head fell a little to the side.

Danny was gone. He was three years old.

I fell on my knees at the edge of his bed and wept bitter tears of repentance. Then and there I surrendered my broken heart, life and soul to Jesus' call and bidding.

Chapter 29

The Führer Finally Leaves

Before Danny's death, I had no faith to support me. In Germany, my family was Lutheran but in name only. I seldom attended church and when I did it was for a wedding, a baptism, or some such occasion for friends of my parents.

Gene's mother had attended and raised Gene in a Baptist church. After he returned home from Europe, Gene again started attending regularly and after our wedding I went with him. However, it was difficult for me to understand or grasp this new teaching and I rejected the Savior's salvation.

Danny's death changed everything. After my change of heart and attitude we decided to regularly attend the Assembly of God Church in Evansville. The fellowship we shared with the pastor and congregation we enjoyed very much.

Nightmares

I've had two episodes of repeating nightmares during my life. As a teenager in Germany, I had a dream that repeated itself many times. In that dream I was being chased by Russian soldiers. After the war, when I had made my way to America, that nightmare ended. I guess I felt safe from the Russians now that I was in the United States. After all, no one could compete with the great United States military. The Americans had the Atomic Bomb and no one else did. The Soviets, or anyone else, would be utter fools to take on the United States.

But after that nightmare left me, another took its place. In the new dream, the nightmarish specter of Adolf Hitler again stood over me, patting me on the head as he had done when I was a child in that summer of 1934, only now in the dream I was an adult.

Gene said he could always tell when I was having the Hitler nightmare. He said I tossed and turned and spoke in German. He couldn't understand what I was saying, but he told me I always spoke the word 'Führer' several times. He would always wake me and save me from Hitler. Of course, neither Gene nor anyone else here in America knew about my blood oath. Despite the happiness my newly found faith gave me, the oath remained to gnaw on my conscience.

But it was God who finally banished Hitler from not just my dreams, but from my life forever.

One day after church service ended, I lingered until everyone had left then I went up front and knelt before the altar. There I prayed and threw my remaining problem at God's feet. I knew only He, in his great mercy, could remove the curse of my blood oath. The heavy weight on my shoulders began to lift from me and a wave of joy and peace flooded over me. God in his own way had spoken to my heart and set me free.

The curse of the blood oath and the Führer's shadow were gone. Adolf Hitler never visited this former BDM group leader again.

Chapter 30

Beyond

Almost a year after my lone, middle-of-the-night arrival in Mount Vernon, Congress's War Bride Act allowed two more German girls to find their destiny in Mount Vernon, this small Indiana town on the Ohio River. And both of them had harrowing escape stories to tell.

Sieglinde Russell (her married surname, and here everyone called her 'Linda') was from Breslau, Germany. Her home town was overrun by the Russians. Her mother was able to escape only days before the fighting over the town began, but Sieglinde and her father were not as lucky. After the city fell, a Russian soldier had his eyes on pretty Sieglinde and grabbed her, intending to have his way with her. Her helpless father stood near and quickly removed his expensive gold wristwatch and showed it to the Russian. That apparently tempted the brute more than Sieglinde and the exchange was made (he could easily find another helpless German victim, but maybe not a watch like this).

That night Sieglinde and her father crawled under a barbed wire fence to safety out of the Russian held area, but not before watching from the trees as the Russians gathered a large group of townspeople into the city square and mowed them down with machine guns.

Elisabeth Dick hailed from Karlsruhe, Germany. Her town was captured by French Moroccan fighters. Their desire for German girls was no different than that of the Russians. As Karlsruhe was being surrounded, many people hid in the caves that dot the hillsides just outside of town. One of the wild Moroccans wanted Elisabeth, but when he saw her crucifix necklace he turned her loose and mumbled something sounding like 'Jesus.' After that, Elisabeth's mother rolled her up in a carpet and hid her in a cave until the French Moroccans moved on.

After they arrived in Mount Vernon, the three of us and our husbands soon became good friends. The men enjoyed exchanging their war stories, and we three girls talked about our soon coming experience of becoming mothers. As fate would have it, as the years went on, each of us raised to adulthood one son and two daughters, all near in age.

The three German girls shared one wonderful experience none of us would ever forget. On April 21, 1952, we proudly stood in line along with a few others in front of a federal judge in Evansville and pledged our allegiance to the United States of America. After five years of proving our sincerity, now we were truly American citizens.

Here in America, everyone except me spelled Elisabeth's name with a 'z' instead of the 's.' She died of cancer in 1966. Linda (Sieglinde) and her husband, Don, moved to Florida early in the new century. She died there a few years later. I think of both Elisabeth and Linda often and still miss them.

Over the years, other Germans found their way to Mount Vernon, but not under the War Bride Act that had expired by the late 1940s. The regular immigration laws were again in effect. However, as far as I know and from what I've been told, I was the first German from the war to arrive in Mount Vernon and in 2017 I will celebrate my 70th year in this wonderful country. Mount Vernon feels like my hometown and I love its good people.

Return to the Fatherland

My first trip back to Germany to visit my parents was in April of 1957—ten years after I watched Vati's lantern disappear into the fog at the Munich train station. I sailed on an ocean liner. Nie wieder! (never again). My seasickness was every bit as bad as my airsickness on my first-ever flight from Frankfurt to Ireland—except the boat trip across the ocean lasted eight days instead of the hours the plane took in 1947. Jets were by now the norm, and they could fly straight through to Frankfurt from the States without refueling. This cut the time down from eight days by ship to about nine hours or so by plane. Subsequently, all my future trips would be by air.

But on this first trip back in '57 I sailed on the German liner *Berlin* from New York City to Bremerhaven, Germany. During my eight days on rolling waves, when I wasn't in the bathroom, I spent a great deal of my time in the game room playing chess with an elderly gentleman from Stuttgart. One game lasted three days. He won that one and strutted about like a peacock (a pure German male reaction).

My Uncle Karl, Mutti's younger brother, picked me up in Bremerhaven in his brand new BMW. Those cars are made in Munich, my home town. Like auto factories in the United States, during the war BMW suspended making cars and instead made engines for the Luftwaffe airplanes. Uncle Karl drove me to Munich, allowing me to see much of the German countryside and many towns and cities along the way. I was surprised and gladdened by the transformation. Unlike Mutti's and my train trip to Hamburg in 1947 to visit my Oma Rath, the Germany I saw outside the car window was now healed, at least when referring to buildings, roads, and other infrastructure. I would learn, however, that the ghosts of the Third Reich still tormented my homeland. Even to this day, these demons linger.

It was wonderful to see my parents, but I found myself homesick for Gene and my children. While I was gone, my darling mother-in-law came to take care of the family.

My next trip back was in 1976, nineteen years later. I took my son Roger's wife, Peggy, their little 3-year-old son (my grandson) and my youngest daughter, Maryhelen, with me. We stayed for three weeks.

Son Roger and I flew to Germany in 1983. He was already a world traveler, having fought with the U.S. Army in Vietnam in the late 60s. Roger enjoyed this trip to Europe very much. He and my Mutti were buddies; she attended his wedding and prayed for him every day while he was in Vietnam. Roger was also a big help to Vati. Together they repaired the fence around the new Dorsch property and felled and sawed up a couple of trees. It was during hot weather and Roger made good use of the genuine Munich beer to quench his thirst.

In 1985, daughter Connie and I rounded out my children's visit to my native land. It was only two weeks before Mutti left us forever. She was 80 years old.

Later, after my Mutti died, I returned to Germany much more often—every other year—to visit and help Vati until he passed away in 1993.

Once, a long time ago, when I found out that the Nazis had euthanized my great aunt, Eliese, I swore revenge. I know now that there is nothing I can do—nothing anyone can do to gain revenge on the Nazis. Their crimes are too staggering to avenge.

I have put off telling the story of my life for decades, so this is certainly not the first biography from a German who lived under the Third Reich. However, I've been told there are very few biographies from former BDM girls, so I hope my 'revenge' is to finally add my name to the list of firsthand witnesses of those dark times and add just one more nail to the coffin of this aberration of history, and refute all those who would deny these things happened.

As of this writing, I am now 86 years old. I have lived a wonderful life in America with a loving husband. I have been blessed with children, grandchildren, and great-grandchildren no one could be prouder of. I have faith that God, in his infinite mercy, has forgiven me for my blood oath to Adolf Hitler. Now, my Christian faith is as irreplaceable to my existence as the air I breathe. The following Psalm has always been one of my favorites. I feel in a way that it was written for me.

He brought me up also out of a horrible pit,
out of the miry clay,
and set my feet upon a rock,
and established my goings.
Psalm 40:2

Epilogue

As of October 2016, Ilse still lives in Mount Vernon, Indiana. At the age of 86, she is physically spry and mentally razor sharp. Her music has stayed by her side. She still plays her accordion at her church in Mount Vernon.

She and Gene Horacek lived a happy married life until Gene's death in April of 1998. He was 77 years old and is buried at Beech Grove Cemetery in Posey County alongside Danny. Ilse will someday lie next to Gene and their son.

Ilse made numerous trips back to Germany while her parents lived. Mutti—Ilse's mother Thea Dorsch—died in 1985. Vati, her father Konrad Dorsch, passed in 1993. Both of Ilse's parents requested that, in death, they be near their only child. Like Gene and Danny, the remains of Konrad and Thea Dorsch are at Beech Grove Cemetery.

As Ilse mentions in the book, she and Gene had four children: Roger, Danny, Connie, and Maryhelen. Connie presented Ilse and Gene with their first grandchildren, twin boys, born in May of 1973. And Connie's would not be the only set of twins. Maryhelen also brought twins into the world, a boy and a girl. Connie would have another son. Roger would have three sons for a total of eight grandchildren for Ilse and Gene. As for great-grandchildren, Ilse likes to say she has 13½ as one is still on the way.

Over the years, Ilse became rather well-known in Mount Vernon for her work translating German letters and documents. The local Historical Society asked her to translate old, long defunct German-language newspapers that appeared in Posey County until 1895 when the newspaper powers-that-be decided to switch to English. Ilse took copious notes when she ran across interesting stories and this eventually led to the Mount Vernon Democrat newspaper asking her to write a weekly column which became quite popular and ran for 25 years, from 1978 until 2003. Ilse eventually published three books of human interest stories from the old German newspapers. She also copied the entire 1880 Posey County census by hand off of micro film—27,000 names with family relationships, places of birth and death, and occupations. This was also published as a book.

So how should we regard the extraordinary life of Ilse Dorsch? I know how I regard it. It's a life full of tragedy, extreme hardships, love, devotion, occasional humor, and triumph. How can one not admire Ilse? Even while growing up in the House of Horrors that was the Third Reich, Ilse kept her humanity. Her life is evidence to the strength of the human spirit, and ultimately a testament to a faith in something greater than one's self.

— Mike Whicker

{Letter from Ilse to Mr. Fisher}

ILSE HORACEK
Mount Vernon, IN 47620

November 25, 2004

Dear Mr. Fisher,

This is a "Thank You" letter — a letter that has been delayed for 57 years. And I can't be sure the Mr. Fisher reading this letter is still you; it may be your son, or even your grandson.

It was July 19, 1947, late at night at the Cincinnati, Ohio, airport. I had just arrived from Germany, by way of New York. I was a 17-year-old "War Bride" on the way to my future husband in Mount Vernon, Indiana. He was supposed to meet me in Cincinnati, but my telegram to him did not reach him in time so I was stranded. The airlines did not know what to do with me. I was an alien under bond and could not be released. I had no American money. Several airline employees huddled behind the ticket counter and discussed my situation. Their attempt to contact Mount Vernon had been unsuccessful.

You stood in line behind me. Your flight to St. Louis was scheduled to leave shortly. When you, a total stranger, became aware of my plight you offered to pay for my ticket to Evansville, Indiana, by way of St. Louis and they allowed you to take me with you. (Today this would hardly be possible and I have wondered if perhaps you were well-known by the airline people.)

Looking back at this happening so long ago, I only remember being totally exhausted, in a strange country after a long trans-Atlantic flight, and having only a limited use of the English language. You became my Good Samaritan. During the flight to St. Louis you gave me enough money to get from Evansville to Mount Vernon and taught me what a half-dollar, a quarter, a dime, a nickel, and a penny were. I did ask you to write your address on a piece of paper so my husband could repay you, which I am sure he did promptly.

I thought of you many times during these years and wanted to thank you personally but the address was lost. I have had a wonderful life here in the Unites States, a happy marriage with a great man, and three successful children. My husband passed away six years ago. Recently I cleaned out his desk and from a stack of letters from his Army buddies fluttered out a yellowed slip of paper: your address from 1947. Only then it was 49 Elwood St. in Newton. On the Internet I found the new one.

And so today I want to thank you for being an angel sent by God to help me when I needed help so long ago. I pray that He has blessed you for it many times.

Thank you and my very best wishes to you,

Sincerely,

Ilse Horacek

PHOTOS

1936. First day of school.
Ilse with her backpack and
cone of treats.

Ilse with her beloved
accordion in the garden of
her home in Gräfelfing,
just outside Munich.

1938. Ilse with her father on holiday
in Austria. The day after this photo
was taken, Hitler's Anschluss, the
takeover of Austria, began.

**1940. Ilse at 10 years old, shortly
before she would enter the Hitler Youth.**

Nov. 1944. Gene Horacek, Ilse's future
husband, in Bastogne, Belgium. One month
later, the Battle of the Bulge would begin and
Bastogne would be surrounded and
under siege by German troops. Gene and the
rest of the American soldiers would hold-on
until the town was relieved by
Patton's 3rd Army.

July 24, 1947. Ilse Dorsch marries Gene Horacek

Gene Horacek during World War II

Ilse becomes a U.S. citizen.

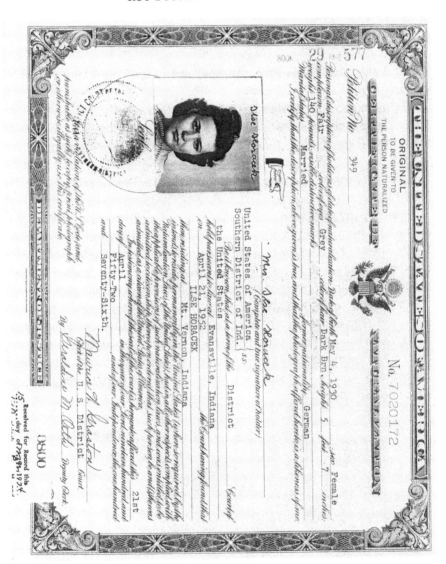

ACKNOWLEDGEMENTS

I must thank David Jones—my attorney, advisor, confidant, and a most valued friend.

My thanks to Tom Lonnberg, Detlef Alle, Kathy Pfettscher, Darrell Davis, David Jones, and David Gray for taking the time to read and review the book. All are lifelong students of history and their opinions hold weight.

A weighty thanks goes to my beloved daughter-in-law, Erin Whicker, a proofreader extraordinaire.

Thanking my wife Sandy is like thanking the captain of a ship. If it weren't for her, none of my books would have been written. Back in the 1990s when I first began writing my first novel *Invitation to Valhalla,* she alone encouraged me to keep writing when others I knew scoffed at the thought of a high school football coach writing a WW II spy novel.

And of course there is Ilse. This is her true story—the story of a life well-lived even in the most trying of circumstances. I was just a guy in the background asking her questions. She was patient enough to endure with good grace my myriad visits to her home, my pestering phone calls, and uncountable emails. That she allowed me to put her story to pen is an honor I could never forget.

— Mike Whicker, 2016

About the Author

A native of Colorado, Mike Whicker now resides in the Midwest.

Novels by Mike Whicker

The Erika Lehmann WW II spy series:
Novel 1: *Invitation to Valhalla*
Novel 2: *Blood of the Reich*
Novel 3: *Return to Valhalla*
Novel 4: *Fall from Valhalla*

and
Proper Suda

Books available at Amazon.com, bn.com,
and on Kindle.

Copies of any of Mike Whicker's books signed by the author are available to be shipped. Copies of *Flowers for Hitler* signed by Ilse Dorsch are also available to be shipped. Contact the author
at email address: mikewhicker1@gmail.com

The author welcomes reader questions and comments.
Email: mikewhicker1@gmail.com

Mike Whicker is also on Facebook

Flowers for Hitler

The Extraordinary Life
of Ilse Dorsch

Flowers for Hitler

CPSIA information can be obtained
at www.ICGtesting.com
Printed in the USA
BVHW01s1934161217
502991BV00001B/98/P